GMT EMEZUE

COMPARATIVE STUDIES IN

AFRICAN DIRGE POETRY

COMPARATIVE STUDIES IN
AFRICAN DIRGE POETRY

by
Gloria Monica T. Emezue
Department of English Language and Literature
University of Ebonyi State
Abakaliki-Nigeria

HANDEL BOOK

AFRICAN DIRGE POETRY
[INTERNATIONAL EDITION]
Copyright © 2001 Gloria Monica. T. Emezue
ISBN: 978-36034-1-8
Cover Design: The Studio Network

All rights reserved. No part of this book may be reproduced, stored in a retrieval system, or transmitted in any form by any means, whether electronic, mechanical, photocopying, recording, or otherwise, without prior written permission of the publishers.

Handel Books Limited
6 Handel Avenue, AI 40003
PO Box 1425 Enugu 40001 Ng WA
E-mail: handelbook@yahoo.co.uk
Website: www.handelbooks.com

A Progeny International project

—▶§◀—

HANDEL BOOKS

COMPARATIVE STUDIES IN
AFRICAN DIRGE
POETRY

*"Probably the most comprehensive study of
African dirge poems by a Nigerian scholar..."*

Gloria Monica Emezue's contribution to research in African literature has led to the submission of a theory of African dirge composition which draws from constant recurring points in that genre of writing. Borne from her conviction that nowhere else in the corpus of oral poetry have there been more works of heightened creative expressions than in dirge poetry, she explores, in this seminal work, the world of various categories of African mourners. They are conjurers of images and weavers of emotions interpreting the human tragic sensitivity with such admirable craftsmanship as can only be known to those gifted bards of all ages and their modern descendants across the continent.

Contents

Preface
Dedication
Acknowledgements

Chapter One

The Poetry of Africa   1
    The Cultural Unity of Africa
    African Poetry and the Idea of Death
    Poetry and the African Heritage
    The social relevance of African poetry

Chapter Two

The Dirge in Africa   16
    The Dirge in Africa
    Dirge Occasion and Performance
    Varying Moods of African Dirge Poems
    Dominant Dirge Motifs
    The African Dirge Structure
    Language of African Dirge

Chapter Three

Igbo Written Traditions   58
    'Uno Onwu Okigbo'
    'Okigbo Ebelebe Egbuole'
    'Odogwu Kabral'

Chapter Four

African Rhythms in English   88
    A Synthesis of Forms
    'Songs for Seers'
    'Lament in a Storm'

'The Story of a Ceylonese Girl'
'Lament for a Dauntless Three'

Chapter Five
Modern Dirge Voices 122
    The Laments of Younger Poets
    Betrayal: 'Letter to Lynda'
    Bitterness: 'Songs of a Marketplace'
    The Acerbity of 'An African Eclipse'
    After-Loss: 'Naked Testimonies'
    Areas of Artistic Convergence

Chapter Six
A Theory of the African Dirge 149
    Dialectical Framework
    Western Patterns, African Structures

Chapter Seven
Summary 170

Figures
1. The 'Total' African Dirge Structure   148
2. Dirge Structure of 'Lament in a Storm'   166
3. Dirge Structure of 'Odogwu Kabral'   168

Select Bibliography 175
Index 180

Preface

This book does not treat those debatable problems or issues regarding our oral traditions. Scholars of African literature have done this with great diligence and merely repeating them here would prove the more tedious and lacklustre. Rather this study of the African dirge tradition is an exploration of the consciousness of artistes and their art in their perception of death as a rite of passage. The communal African psyche has come to retain a deeply philosophical outlook in face of natural and man-made disasters. When expressed through the creative disciplines, this world view emerges in an elaborate fusion of artistry and individuality worthy of serious study.

We have seen such artistic progression especially in Chinua Achebe's works marking a creative enterprise that spans the colonial experience inscribing our decades of struggles with those committed voices that echo through our continent's successions of political and economic turbulence. Africa's songs, poetry, drama, dance, rhythm, sculpture and craft have all been expressions of her varied emotions in different epochs of her traumatic history.

The African ontology is one that is usually cognitive of a

spiritual world of ancestors from where, it is believed, the departed fathers preside over the affairs of the living. Nowhere, perhaps, in the corpus of traditional poetry have there been more works of heightened feelings than in the dirge. The gloomy circumstances of death give vent to poetry of unusual intensity and spontaneity. Here, the mourner becomes a poet in his own right; he is a conjurer of images and a weaver of emotions aimed toward not only the full realisation of the dirge sentiment but also the expurgation of overwhelming feelings. Other incidents akin to the death include the loss of a loved one, the atrophy of dreams, war, disaster, political betrayals and even some instances of human treachery.

These emotional responses elicit what may be called the communal consciousness which the bard evokes in his despair, frustration, loss, desolation and isolation at the instance of the death. What is almost always realised at dirge renditions and performances might be the sense of shared responsibility and the effect of general catharsis.

Adopting the methodical and investigative approach, I have set out to portray the role and function of African dirge songs in their communities. Moving from the general (African milieu) through the specific (Igbo) and contemporary local (Nigerian) situations, I have drawn some deductions and generalisations concerning the dirge in Africa. The major choice of dirge songs, both oral and written, and of poets has been, except with few exceptions, restricted to the Ibo. Thus Igbo society has largely served my paradigm for Africa.

Furthermore, I have looked at both modes of 'written' and 'oral' poetic expressions. Exploring the written dirge works of Chinua Achebe, Emeka Chimezie and R.M Ekechukwu helps establish the link between oral and written traditions of African art riding on the crest of indigenous languages. It is significant that modern African writers, using the language of English, have advanced a literature of simultaneous oral and modern traditions. The poems of Pol Ndu, T.C Nwosu, and Ossie Enekwe are used to illustrate the oral nuances of speech, idioms, proverbs and imagery in the larger heritage of African dirge poetry.

A younger generation of African poets has been included in this study using some important voices in recent Nigerian poetry who employ the tone of lamentation in delineating the seasons of atrophy that plague their national progress. From their acute awareness of history emerges a threnodic voice that has now become part of modern African art and holds much relevance in contemporary national literatures.

A theory of the African dirge, with distinct features from its western counterpart has been provided by this research. This has been given graphic representation to achieve a sense of form and clarity. The intention is not towards the problematic ingenuity of a scholarly prescription, certainly not to advance a paradigm by which an artiste's creative impulse must flow. We can therefore approach the issue of theory with as much caution as a true literary critic employs while eliciting the merits of a work of art. Perhaps, a better term would still remain *features* as against theor*y*. But in as much as any African dirge poem reveals some degree of adherence to the observed patterns of creative expression, I would be satisfied that my research effort would have yielded its true and original intentions.

GMT

Dedication

This is for Z
And those beings who helped

Acknowledgements

From inception of this project, I am grateful to two men: Professor Sunday O. Anozie, whose useful guidance got me started on this quest for the authentic African dirge tradition, and Professor Winifred Feuser (of blessed memories) for his friendship and inspiring words when we first met at the University of Port Harcourt in 1989. It is my wish that this book goes a little measure to express a scholar's gratitude for all they did for African literature, the latter especially in the field of translations. I would wish that Feuser's contributions to Africa and her literatures (along with Ulli Beier's and others) should continue to inspire cross cultural literary studies in the years to come.

It is also in this spirit that I am quite grateful to Professors Onuora Ossie Enekwe of the Institute of African Studies, University of Nigeria and C. T. Maduka of the University of Port Harcourt who both assisted me very much towards establishing some validity for this research.

Indeed the completion of this work owes much debt to these and many other friends and confidantes too numerous to mention. At every turn, Chi has always been there for me. He always had a way of turning up when he was most needed. His suggestions and editing went a long way in moulding this project to fruition.

Coming nearer home, there is mum: writer, critic, and traditional bard fondly called *PK* by friends and who inspired most of my writings and academic quests in life. What's more, Mummy had always kept a loving heart and an agile memory for us, her children. This is thanking her for being the kind woman she is.

To our little Handel I remain most grateful for crying the times he did. Here's also to my 'buster' twins, Nefertiti and CJ, who came at the completion of this book. I remain very grateful for their co-operation in all that we did, or could not do, together. To my sister, Ifeoma, I say thanks for trying to do your best for us all.

GMT

Chapter 1

The Poetry of Africa

*The cultural unity of Africa * African poetry and the idea of death * Poetry and the African heritage *The social relevance of African poetry*

The Cultural Unity of Africa

Africa, as one of the largest continents of the world, is the home of the people of the dark race. Despite its large geographical expanse and several languages, it has been noted that much of the cultures found in African societies are similar. Most writers on Africa agree on this uniformity. According to Kofi Awoonor,

> African traditional society ...have all been shaped by a fairly unified historical experience, shared cultural impacts from external sources, and above all, by a large degree of interaction of one culture with another.[1]

---

[1] Kofi Awoonor, *The Breast of the Earth*, New York: NOK Publishers International, 1975, p.49

This interaction of cultures can be traced to Africa's high degree of nomadic life that is characterised by migrations. It has been suggested that in some time past, the people that dwelled in the high mountain areas of Africa had dealings and contact with the people of the valleys and grasslands, and vice versa, thus resulting in common cultural affiliations.

Yet Africa is not just a structural or geo-physical entity. Chinua Achebe rightly notes that Africa is much more than geography: it is (even more importantly) a metaphysical landscape.

> It is in fact a view of the world and of the whole cosmos perceived from a particular position.[2]

In the Oduduwa myth which summarises the origin of the Yoruba, for instance, Ife is portrayed as the spiritual centre of humanity. This common ancestry and shared experience go a long way in affirming the Yoruba brotherhood across the whole of West Africa and the diaspora.

Similarly, history records the common experience of

---

[2] Chinua Achebe, *Morning Yet on Creation Day*, London: Heinemann Educational Books Ltd, 1975, p.50

the Trans-Saharan trade by the people of North Africa and their Western counterparts. While the Trans-Saharan trade was a historical rallying point for the people of Africa, the Trans-Atlantic (slave) trade conversely marked a major avenue for the scattering of the people across the continents of the world.

Of significance therefore in the nomadic lifestyles and migrations of the tribes of Africa is the cross-culturalisation of the continent and her peoples over the decades. Despite linguistic differences which is a feature of African tribal societies, the cultural similarity remains an unbroken thread which links her peoples. A close look at the distribution of people in Africa today would, in the words of Awoonor,

> ...reveal a great degree of unity in concept and practice among what had hitherto been regarded as vastly different people and culture.[3]

These include such practices as the institution of chieftaincy, belief in the divinity of chiefs, rulers and village heads. Others are belief in, and sometimes worship of, ancestors (traditional animism), observance of initiatory

---

[3] Kofi Awoonor, 1975, p.5

rites (from birth to death), nature and power of kinship based on blood, the idea of a supreme creator who rules through minor gods and deities, including a largely metaphysical concept of the world. All these were common values at some time in the past. They are responsible for the cultural similarity that exists within communities all over the African continent thus forming that 'metaphysical landscape' which distinguishes the continent and its progeny from the rest of the world.

African poetry and the idea of Death

Most African dirge compositions retain identical features throughout the continent. An African dirge is a song of mourning composed and rendered for a departed relative, friend or colleague. The variables of composition may lie in the manner and method of rendition. But the attitude to death draws from the people's philosophy of life, the place of the African in relation to his world of the living, the dead and the unborn. This African ontological worldview affirms the trinity of the dead, the living and the yet unborn as the eternal cyclic order in which the rites of passage of the living form only an infinitesimal journey or stage.

Death is therefore interwoven in life, as breathing is

in living. Death expresses the general links between the past and the present, the living and the dead. It is believed that before an individual could move into the abode of the great ancestors, the necessary rites of passage from birth to death must be observed.[4]

African philosophy is cognisant that life does not end with death. This belief in life after death goes far back to Ancient Egyptian times some five thousand years ago. Egypt was not only the cradle of one of the greatest civilisations that the world ever witnessed, it is the origin of the present world civilisations. From the Egyptian *Book of the Dead*, the ancient collection of texts that contain instructions for life after death, we have some fascinating poetic evocations as these:

> I am the great god who begets Himself.
> The Secret might of my name
> Creates the heavenly order of the gods.
> The gods do not impede my progress.
> I am yesterday.
> I know tomorrow.
> The fierce battle the gods fight
> With one another
> Takes place according to my will.
> …
> O world egg, hear me!

---

[5] Erich Von Daniken, *In Search of Ancient Gods*, London: Souvenir Press Ltd, 1974, pp 14-15

> I am Horus of millions of years.
> I am Lord and master of the throne.
> Freed from evil, I traverse the ages
> And spaces that are endless.[5]

Horus, the Egyptian hawk-headed sun god is much like a judicial deity before whom the soul of the dead must come for judgement. The immensity of Horus' power is impressed on the subjects, much as Jehovah's to Christian believers. But even of more significance is the propitiation made to the god of the sun on behalf of the dead. This traverses all spatial demarcations in the eternal intercourse of human and divine existence.

Igbo philosophy holds life as a sacred continuum of the world of the living and that of 'spiritland' —the world of the dead. Says Achebe,

> This 'spiritland' where dead ancestors recreate a life comparable to their earthly existence is not only parallel to the human world but is also similar and physically contiguous with it for there is constant coming and going between them in the endless traffic of life, death and reincarnation.[6]

---
[6] Chinua Achebe, 1975, p.95

Poetically, this coming and going is akin to a busy market. A famous women dance group illustrates this in a song:

> Anyi biara abia n'elu uwa a
> Uwa anyi no n'ime ya abughi nke anyi o
> Ihe anyi biara n'elu uwa o bu ahia nu o
> Uwa bu onye zuru nke ya 'la nu o
> Elu uwa bu ahia
>
> We are visitors upon the earth
> This world does not belong to us
> We have come to buy and sell
> And afterwards will go home[7]
> (Translation by the author)

The symbolic market in this song is the earth upon which our 'buying and selling' therefore assumes an apt representation of daily rigours and other exigencies. When our time is up, we pass into the land of the ancestors. Some take their place among the revered ones if their life on earth was meritorious. Yet while there, they are still united to the living by blood. This is because

> blood, being the most meaningful

---

[7] Nkwerre Women Dance Group in Igboland, Nigeria WA

> force for the living, also unites them to the dead...[for] no family [really] diminishes. The ancestors become minor deities in the spiritual hierarchy.[8]

The idea of ancestors as deities stretches as far back as Ancient Egypt and beyond. Since Egyptian religious tradition held the king as deity, at death the king was carefully preserved (mummified) for it was believed that he would make use of the body again in a subsequent incarnation. Ancient Sumerian legends also spoke of gods who dwelt among men and left behind their great knowledge and wisdom promising to return some day.[9]

Whereas the king would re-incarnate in the same body in Egypt of the ancient times, in a kind of corporeal return, the ancestor-deities in some parts of Africa would one day return in a new body. The identifiable links between this 'new person' and the late ancestor may be hidden behind recognisable behavioural traits, which the latter had exhibited during his previous life on earth.

But as long as the dead ancestor is still living in the world of the dead, sacrifices are offered and appeals made to him in times of trouble and peace. This traditional poem from Congo illustrates the relationship between the African

---

[8] Kofi Awoonor, 1975, p. 50
[9] Erich von Daniken, *Chariots of the Gods? Was God an astronaut?* London: Corgi Books, 1980 pp. 40 - 41

son and his departed ancestor who transmutes into the guardian ancestral spirit of the home.

> I have held out my hands to you
> And he who holds out his hand dies not
> I have shown you the animals for the feast
> And I have brought you no other presents
> Except palm wine
> That you may favour the procreation of wealth
> And here are the kola nuts I brought you ...[10]

Here the ancestor is in a revered spiritual state, yet the son's approach, albeit with a sombre sense of deference, portrays the homestead familiarity between son and paterfamilias.

From Ghana we have the following rendition that appears quite familiar with African literary tradition:

> Agosu if you go tell them,
> Tell Nyidevu, Kpeti, and Kove
> That they have done us evil;
> Tell them their house is falling
> And the trees in the fence
> Have been eaten by termites;

---

[10] Ruth Finnegan, *Oral Literature in Africa*, Nairobi: Oxford University Press, 1970, p.184

> That the martels curse them.
> Ask them why they idle there
> While we suffer, and eat sand,
> And the crow and the vulture
> Hover always above our broken fences
> And strangers walk over our portion.[11]

The poet is instructing a newly departed relative to admonish their ancestors who have not lived up to expectations of the living. This sense of wrong or ill treatment probably stems from a nonchalant attitude of the ancestors over the affairs of the living. The ancestors failed to do their duty by the living, and the latter have fallen victims of the colonists dwelling among them. Although the line of communication is unidirectional as in some religious addresses, yet in African communal interactions, the son (worshipper) enjoys this direct communication (in his complaints) with his gods (ancestors who have treated them badly or slacked in their duty).

Poetry and the African Heritage

Modern African poetic heritage incorporates both written and oral traditional forms of expression. This heritage, as in African literature, is as old as the continent itself. Records of its written forms are traceable to Pyramid texts of ancient Egypt five thousand years ago has been

---

[11] D. I. Nwoga ed., *West African Verse,* United Kingdom: Longman Group Limited, 1982, p. 75

noted. By implication therefore, African poetic heritage is older than European poetry by some two thousand years. Thus African literature as a whole has exercised some influences on many of later world civilisations. The Aesop's tales of Ethiope, for example, were later taken to Europe where it nourished the literary tradition of Ancient Greece.[12]

Today, traditional African poetry (which is mostly the oral form of poetic expression) still co-exists with and enriches its modern counterparts, thus offering a wealth of poetry that reflects all aspects of life. Their study, as Egudu and Nwoga have suggested with regard to African (Igbo) poetry should pertain to

> the exposition of its merits by its intrinsic nature as poetry of high quality and an expression of a people's history, their varied belief and their states of mind and emotion[13]

The term 'modern' African poetry has been viewed

---

[12] Chinweizu, *Voices from Twentieth Century Africa*, London: Faber and Faber, 1988, Introduction. Also see Cheik Anta Diop, *The African Origin of Civilisation,* Westport, Connecticut, Lawrence Hill & Company, 1974, p xv.

[13] R. N Egudu and D.I Nwoga ed. *Poetic Heritage: Igbo Traditional Verse,* London: Heinemann Educational Books Ltd, 1973 (Preface)

by scholars as mostly poems written by Africans expressing African sensibilities in European languages or the language of the colonisers. This form of poetry on its own has always been committed. Its early fathers like L.S Senghor, Gladys May Casely-Hayford, Raphael Ernest Grail Armattoe, Michael Dei-Anang, Dennis Brutus, Dennis Osadebay and, David Diop sought to project an image of Africa which was both experiential and idyllic. In most cases it grew as a response to colonial and racial supremacist attitudes.

It was Aristotle who sought to distinguish between history and poetry and concluded that poetry in dealing with the universal rather than the particular was more philosophic and higher in nature than history. But African poetry is not only universal in its pre-occupation; it also deals with historical particulars such as racism, colonialism, Negritude, neo-colonialism, corruption and regular military interventions.

Much as African poetics arise from deeply felt emotional feelings, issues of functionality are not discounted. Rather it is this *need* that underlines the commitment of African poetry and African art. It is essentially a historical need that can range from such human experiences as death, birth or such memorable encounters as colonial rule, capitalism and racism; the latter which led to the rise of Negritude as a philosophic and artistic ideology of African poetry. With Negritude, the black man can 'penetrate the sources of life itself by embracing life through sympathy. It is metaphysical or agricultural and contrasted or opposed to what Sartre calls an 'engineer's prose' [14]

This distinction appears to serve solely the purpose of ideological movements. The position of African poetry in its total indigenous contemporaneity spans all spheres of activity. It is as Merveille Herskovits says of aboriginal oral art as being:

> a valid expression of the creative imagination, channelled by a sophisticated assessment of man and his relation to the world in which he lives. [15]

However, the world in which he lives is a changing world, from early agrarian stages of development through the colonial and post-colonial periods in history all of which

---

[14] Renate Zahar, *Colonialism and Alienation*, Benin City: Ethiope Publishing Corporation, 1974, p.63

[15] Jacob Drachler, *African Heritage*, New York: Collier Books, 1964 (Preface)

witnessed the various stages of protest, nationalism, revolutionary and other social themes.

The evolution of African poetry out of the co-existence of the oral and the written form in mutually acceptable and correlative whole is in line with the idea of progress as T. S Eliot had argued:

> time present and time past
> ...[are] present in time future/and time future contained in time past.[16]

Thus having rescued his past from colonial rationalism the African poet also realises that the past is not one of those museum pieces in which its literary heritage would seem to rust in arcane sanctity. Rather the past co-exists with the present and both share in the prospects of time future. By this discovery, he has therefore answered the question posed by Jacob Drachler decades ago. Will the new intellectuals find the traditional oral literature usable?[17] Drachler had asked. The answer today is without doubt, in the affirmative.

---

[16] John Hayward ed., *Selected Prose: T.S Eliot*, Victoria, Penguin Books Ltd, 1963, p.4

[17] Jacob Drachler, 1964 (Introduction)

The social relevance of African poetry

The relevance of African poetry to its communal needs and times has further consolidated this positive affirmation to Drachler's question. African poetry (whether written in indigenous or foreign language or in its oral form) originates in all sorts of sacred and secular contexts and is truly an every day matter. Despite the 'modernising forces,' which are believed to have destroyed African customs, the fact remains that the dialogue with the past was never totally broken. The African has always been in spiritual alignment with his god. After all, what the African had garnered from the 'civiliser' as J.P Ajayi reminds us,

> was not a substitute education but a supplement, a system of apprenticeship by which the children acquired additional arts and skills; the art of reading and writing, gauging palm oil, or manufacturing gun-powder, or sugar or building boats.[18]

African poetry, like its religion, integrates with the African way of life and is committed to serving a purpose in public affairs and other common needs in the society, be it

---

[18] J.F.A Ajayi, *Christian Missions in Nigeria 1841 - 1891*, London: Longman Books Ltd, 1965, p. 133

emotional, social or physical. In the whole range of contemporary oral poetry in indigenous African languages, we find a variety of social and religious preoccupations with love, marriage, life, death, war, hunting, hunger, and fate. There are songs and prayers in supplication to the deity or in expression of poetic feelings in times of joy and celebration, mourning and disaster, etc. All these make African poetry not only complete in its expressive exigency but also dynamic in most contemporary situations as we shall see later.

Chapter 2

The Dirge in Africa

The dirge in Africa *Occasion and Performance *Varying moods of African dirge poems *Dominant dirge motifs *The African dirge structure *Language of African dirge

The dirge in Africa

The foundation of all African literatures is the African oral tradition. ... African literature embodies the literary aspects of African oral performances. From these grow the roots of African life, culture and world view.[1]

Frequently the tragedy of human loss and destruction elicits a great need to 'sing.' Lamentation becomes a precious outlet for the gnawing spirit. In this Beninoise 'Song for the Dead,' themes of loss and separation run through the dirge.

> I came to drink with my friend
> And find him I could not

---

[1] E.N Emenyonu, *The Rise of the Igbo Novel*, Ibadan, Oxford University Press, 1978, p. 2

> O death, who taketh away life
> And giveth no day at court...²

From a traditional viewpoint the incidence of death is as sacred rite. It furnishes a special occasion for its rendition at funeral ceremonies to honour a departed one. It is marked by the preponderance of mixed emotions borne from a communal response to tragedy.

Consequently, the African dirge is one of the elevated forms of poetry. The emotional base of poetic feelings informs its universal appeal. Edith Ihekwazu agrees with this idea. 'Poetry does require craft,' she says, 'but it has its roots in genuine emotions. It is a way of overcoming and controlling emotions by giving them form.'³

This is particularly true of the dirge and its performance in Africa. Inspired by the intrinsically emotional feeling, the dirge composition also needs high creative imagination and intellectual discrimination while evoking the tragic mood to make the final effect wholly cathartic.

This nineteenth century Moari song of mourning by

---

[2] Jacob Drachler, 1964, p. 61

[3] Ossie Enekwe, *Broken Pots*, New York, Greenfield Review Press, 1977, Preface

Te Heuheu Herea helps illustrate the deep emotional outburst of a fully realised dirge.

> Many women call on me to sleep with them
> But I'll have none so worthless and so wanton
> There is not one like Rangiaho, so soft to feel
> Like a small, black eel
> I would hold her again
> Even the wood in which she lies;
> But like the slender flax stem
> She slides from the first to the second heaven
> The mother of my children
> Gone
> Blown by the wind
> Like a spume of a wave
> Into the eye of the void.[4]

We are struck by the beauty of Rangiaho, her rare feminine qualities poised against the sudden loss 'blown by the wind/like a spume of a wave/into the eye of the void' evoke tragic departure which we are compelled to share and identify with. Drawn along the mode of a dirge sentiment, this poem is best realised in performance, the ceremony dramatised by the mourner holding on to the coffin of his beloved wife: 'I would hold her again/even the wood in which she lies.' But the final reality of her passage from 'first'

---

[4] B. Mitcalfe, *Poetry of the Maori*, Hamilton and Auckland, Paul's Book Arcade, 1961, p. 20

to 'second heaven' elicits the painful disappointment, 'Gone....'

The dirge, as a fully realised poetic tradition, serves the enigmatic purpose of providing a creative avenue through which personal sorrow and frustration could be made a collective experience resolved by purging our sentiments of all emotions that beleaguer them. It is as Ernest Fisher says of art as having its origin in magic since man masters in art what he cannot master in life. The dirge in Africa takes its magical role as a collective ritual process in overcoming the sickness of tragic depression. By this observation, there can be no pretensions as to the functionality of art in their traditional or modern cultural settings.

Dirge Occasion and Performance

African burials, funerals and memorials serve as occasions to share, mourn and also celebrate a rite of passage. The occasion is communal, but above all it serves as a period for ablution of tragic personal and group memories. At instances of death, the relatives of the deceased gather to mourn and lament if the person dies in his prime. They tend to mark an elaborate celebration if the person dies at a very old age. Why the death of a young one is hardly celebrated is because in most parts of Africa it is tantamount to taboo for the old to bury the young. The ineluctable rite is usually marked, but the funfair that normally accompanies that of the aged is absent.

Death songs (*abu onwu*) among the Igbo (like most other communities in Africa) are sung at death, burial and funeral or memorial ceremonies. Burial ceremonies or funerals in most parts of Igboland is an elaborate affair. This stems from the idea that the people are celebrating a rite of passage. As a result all the necessary observances, dances and performances that need be performed must take place before the body is interred.

An African perspective informs and sustains the communal interaction. In Igboland, funeral ceremonies may witness a large turn-out of sympathisers who may be relatives of the deceased, his age-grade members, the different farming, hunting or fishing guilds to which he belongs, in addition to a host of invisible partakers of this communion from beyond the dead and unborn.

Some occasions for the rendition of these dirges vary. Sometimes the dirge commences as soon as the mourner receives news confirming the death. In this song the bereaved wife mourns her husband:

> They had the flesh and I have the bones
> The lucky ones had the flesh
> Ants have eaten my Nkrishi
> My torch bearer has gone

> He is gone forever
> Pussy cat
> Hunting dog
> Who arrests empty-handed[5]

At other times, after the news of death is relayed, relatives gather to fix a date for the funeral. The services of an experienced mourner, who is a specialist in the art of funeral rendition, will be sought by the family or the guilds to which the deceased belonged. The leader of this team becomes the weeping poet, so to say. Also during funeral ceremonies, as Finnegan notes, dirges are sung round the corpse or

> (a)round the house in which the corpse lies, while it is being prepared for burial. Sometimes, this is followed by a period of public mourning during which the corpse lies in state and dirges are sung.[6]

Usually while the body is being prepared for burial, the mourner is at work in praise of the deceased and giving accounts of the good deeds of the hero. M.F Ganyi cites an

---

[5] Mowang F Ganyi, 'In-Performance Composition in Bakor Song Texts: A view of the Parry-Lord Oral Formalaic Theory', in E.N Emenyonu ed., *Critical Theory and African literature*, Ibadan, Heinemann Educational Books, 1987, pp.157-8

[6] Ruth Finnegan, 1970, p. 147

instance of the funeral of a world war veteran who dies during a squabble over land,

> Hum Kirr
> The little one
> Who sits on a tiger's head.
> King of the jungle
> How could you have died
> During a grass-hopper hunt?[7]

The aim here might have been to induce heart-rending sorrow and full sense of tragedy. The mourner, through other emotive gestures like touching the feet, face and hands of the deceased, sustains the lament before the corpse is laid to rest.

During performance or realisation, the poet has the exceptional task of heightening and sustaining audience interest in the lament through period of mourning. Some Igbo burial traditions organise the funeral occasion to last three, seven, twenty-one or forty days. This depends on the age and social status of the deceased. If he was a titled notable, then more days would be spent in mourning. During this period of burial and funeral celebration, it is the duty of the poet-mourner to sustain the interest of the audience in the

---

[7] Mowang F Ganyi, 1987, p. 145

lament.

After a full cycle –usually twelve months– a ceremony is normally conducted to mark final memorial rites for the deceased. During this period, which is more of a celebration, the poet has the duty of creating varied moods for the occasion. His performance helps the audience to relax, or, he tries to create wistful memories depending on the mood of his lament. For the funeral ceremony of a revered old man, a rendition of the following kind of dirge after interment may not quite be out of place:

> You have come to the festival,
> Men and women.
> Of quarrelsome people, let there be none among you.
> The husband who has brought his wife
> Must spend with her the night in the same place
> He who has no wife
> Shall not take one belonging to someone else.
> My whole village, I have pacified
> He who has the mastery over fetishes
> Let him leave them in his own village.
> If anyone wants to prowl at night like a witch,
> Let him beware, our fetishes will make him jump.
> It will be said: he has eaten bad food at the festival,
> In truth, he will have devoured his own self.
> He who is very hungry,
> Let him not take food by force;

Let him ask for it, and he shall be satisfied...

The pervading mood at this instance, although triggered by death, is that of feasting and merriment. The dead man, adopting the voice of the bard in first person narrative admonishes his relatives and other guests on the proper code of behaviour for the burial. Even the dead is not at all acrimonious at the idea of celebration and jocundity, but is rather concerned that the festivity should go smoothly.

> He who wishes to dance,
> Let him dance to the drum he prefers.
> But let no one pick a quarrel.
> I have convoked all of you,
> I want you to return home in peace.
>
> (Bakongo Zaire and Angola) [8]

Varying moods of African dirge poems

From the creative virtuosity of the dirge poet, several of these moods are created in a dirge rendition.

Frustration and Helplessness

The preoccupation of most dirges is that of loss and separation while the mood is filled with sorrow and sadness. At other times the feelings progress into deep-seated frustration and helplessness as can be drawn from this

---

[8] Chinweizu, *Voices from Twentieth-Century Africa*, London, Faber and Faber, 1988, p. 307

Togolese dirge entitled 'The Beautiful Playground'

> The beautiful playground goes quickly to ruin,
> The beautiful game field goes quickly to ruin,
> Dense jungle soon becomes grass steppe, grass steppe,
> Our beautiful town returns to open plain,
> Our beautiful town returns to open plain.
>
> Let the grave-diggers not bury me,
> Let one bury my feet and leave my body free;
> So that my kindred may come and see my face,
> Come and look in my face.
>
> The drum does not beat to joy,
> The drum does not beat to joy,
> 'Misery, misery,' beats the drum,
> Only to misery the drum beats
>
> If death were game, a hunter would kill him, and I would be given a thigh
> Would kill him, and I would be given a thigh,
> A hunter would kill him, and I would be given an arm,
> The slayer of my dear father,
> A hunter would kill him, and I would be given an arm,
> The slayer of my dear mother,
> A hunter would kill him, and I would be given an arm,
> The slayer of my dear brother.
> Could not King Death be a game animal, so that a hunter would kill him and I be given a thigh?
> (Ewe Togo)[9]

---

[9] Chinweizu, 1988, p. 301

In Ewe tradition, a damage caused by an ox is duly compensated with a gift of that ox's thigh whenever the animal was killed. In this song therefore, the persona feels that he has been wronged by death and deserves the appropriate compensation. But the impossibility of death to be killed by a hunter is what creates the sense of frustration. The futility of the act of killing death is contrastingly aggravated by the awareness of the destruction that death has wrecked on his family;

> The slayer of my dear father
> ...
> The slayer of my dear mother
> ...
> The slayer of my dear brother

The final rhetorical question helps to seal the helplessness of the situation. The poet wails: 'Could not King Death be a game animal, so that a hunter would kill him and I be given a thigh?'

Bitterness and Anger

The feeling of bitterness stems from the acute loneliness which is the inescapable feeling that follows the passing away of a beloved. The idea of being left 'all alone' (abandoned) is expressed in 'Ikwa uwa' ('Sorrow') where the poet-persona compares himself to a parcel of meat left over the fire to roast.

Sometimes feelings of bitterness and anger are aroused in view of the deprivations and suffering that bog the survivors consequent upon the death of a relative. This Ugandan traditional poem best illustrates this attitude.

> If death were not there,
> Where would the inheritor get things?
> The cattle have been left for the inheritor;
> Ee, how would the inheritor get things?
> The iron-roofed house has been left for the inheritor;
> Ee, if death were not there,
> How would the inheritor get rich?
> The bicycle has been left for the inheritor;
> ...
> A wife has been left for the inheritor;
> Ee, inheritor, how would you have lived?
> The house has been left for the inheritor;
> If death were not there,
> How would the inheritor get things?
>
> (Acholi Uganda)
> Translated by Okot p'Bitek.[10]

While death impoverishes some people, it might make

---

[10] Chinweizu, 1988, p. 311

others rich, e.g., embalmers, coffin makers, wine sellers or the surviving inheritors. In traditional societies and even in contemporary communities, inheritance of property may be patrilineal or matrilineal and has little or nothing to do with legal a declaration (writing a will) or bequeathing of property. In the above poem therefore, we note items such as 'cattle,' 'iron-roofed house,' 'bicycle,' and 'wife,' which a relative who goes by the derogatory name of 'inheritor' would take possession of. The poet-persona is quite angry at death, while simultaneously satirising the 'inheritor' who is portrayed as being indolent.

Loss and Uprootment

In *'Ikwa uwa'* (Sorrow), the beginning line 'death has crushed my heart' transports the sense of loneliness to despair and despondency. The theme of loss and uprootment is explored in the following lines:

> *Nwannem emeli egbuelem onwu*
> *Nwannem alaputam n'ezi gbali ito*
> *Nwannem akwabam aya ka ngiga*
> *Mana ngiga kusili aya ma hu onye metulu ya aka*
> *Onwu abuam ka-ede, kaa m'ana*
> *Aka ekpe aga mu na'azu Onwu emeem okponu*
> *Ugegbe m'awa*
> *Nkem agaa* [11]

---

[11] R. N Egudu and D.I Nwoga ed., 1973, p. 136

> My brother death has crushed my heart
> My brother has left me at cross roads
> My brother has left me hanging over the fire like
>
> a parcel of meat to dry
> But a parcel of meat over the fire will still have
>
> somebody to touch it
> Death has reaped me like cocoyam and peeled
>
> off my tubers
> My left hand has turned to my back
> Death has turned me into bitterness itself
> My mirror is broken
> My life is gone.
> (Translation by Egudu and Nwoga)

In this wailing song, the mourner expresses his bitterness and a profound sense of frustration. The images are primarily those of desolation, pain and (a feeling of) 'uprootment.' These serve to accelerate the feeling of loneliness.

> ...
> *alaputam na ezi gbalu ito*
> ...
> *akwubam aya ka ngiga*
> *Ugegbe m'awa*
> *Nkem agaa*
> ...

> left at the cross roads
> ...
> left hanging over the fire like a parcel of meat to dry
> My mirror is broken
> My life is gone

The mourner searches for appropriate epithets to describe his agony, but even the image of roasting is not adequate because, as he says, 'even a parcel of meat over fire will still have/somebody to touch it.' Hence, he looks for more concrete images:

> ... abuam k'ede,
> aka ekpe agaa mu n'azu
> emeem okponu
> (... uprooted me like cocoyam
> my left hand twisted to my back
> turned me into bitterness itself.)

Poetic vividness is achieved through striking similes which are more powerfully evoked here than would have been achieved under different circumstances. Death, in its irreparability and hopelessness, is seen as a harbinger of ultimate doom and destruction.

The sense of Inevitability (Destiny)

The sense of inevitability creates the mood of surrender and acceptance. Based on the philosophical attitude to life and the idea of continuation of existence in the spiritual worlds, death is accepted as an inevitable companion of man that must come when it will. Therefore lamentation, sometimes, is not at the instance of death (although death will come one day) but at the suddenness and unobtrusive way in which it arrives. This Ugandan dirge *'When Death comes to fetch you'* illustrates an acceptance of the inevitability of the tragic destiny:

> It is true
> White man's medicines are strong
> But Acoli medicines
> Are also strong.
>
> The sick gets cured
> Because his time has not yet come:
> But when the day has dawned
> For the journey to Pagak
> No one can stop you,
> White man's medicines
> Acoli medicines,
> Crucifixes, rosaries,
> Toes of edible rats,
> The horn of the rhinoceros
> None of them can block the path
> That goes to Pagak!

When Death comes
To fetch you
She comes unannounced,
She comes suddenly
Like the vomit of dogs,
And when She comes
The wind keeps blowing
The birds go on singing
And the flowers
Do not hang their heads.
The agoga bird is silent
The agoga comes afterwards,
He sings to tell
That Death has been that way!

When Mother Death comes
She whispers
Come,
And you stand up
And follow
You get up immediately,
And you start walking
Without brushing the dust
On your buttocks.

You may be behind
A new buffalo-hide shield
And at the mock fight
Or in battle
You may be matchless;

You may be hiding
In the hole
Of the smallest black insect,
Or in the darkest place
where rats breast-feed their puppies,
or behind the Agoro hills,

You may be the fastest runner,
A long-distance runner,
But when Death comes
To fetch you
You do not resist
You must not resist,
You cannot resist!

Mother Death
She says to her little ones,
Come!
Her little ones are good children,
Obedient, Loyal,
And when Mother Death calls
Her little ones jump,
They jump gladly
For she calls
And offers simsim paste
Mixed with honey!
She says
My only child
Come, come let us go.
Let us go
And eat white ants' paste
Mixed with shea-butter!

And who can resist that?

White diviner priests,
Acoli herbalists,
All medicine men and medicine women
Are good, are brilliant
When the day has not yet dawned
For the great journey
The last safari
To Pagak

Okot p'Bitek (Uganda) Excerpt from Song of Lawino [11]

Death comes quietly and silently, sings the poet; it descends quickly and suddenly to call its victim and the called has no choice but follow immediately. There is no escape, no hiding place for anybody once the time to go to 'pagak' arrives. Pagak in this poem is a euphemism for the land of the dead. Death is personified as ('she') an understanding and very good mother, who calls on her children to follow her when she deems the time appropriate for the final journey. She does not need to beat them to compel obedience; she entices them to her.

Dominant dirge motifs

Motifs are sub themes or ideas that are recurrent in a work of art. Different motifs are discernible in the African dirge. Most prominent of them are the motifs of search and

---

[11] Chinweizu, 1988, p. 302

journey.

Search

The sense of loss felt at the departure of a loved one is heightened by the motif of search. In 'Anyi-na-acho' ('We are searching') for example, the mourners all go out in different directions in search of the departed person. While singing the song, a search is conducted around the areas that the deceased usually frequented. This dramatic enacting of the song helps in bringing out its meaning. As Lord rightly notes, actual performance aids the composition of most oral poems. 'Performance (often) depended on a special technique of composition to facilitate the rapid narration'.[12]

'*Onye k'anyi na-acho,*' another popular dirge poem, has almost become a prototype of the search motif.

O bu onye k'anyi na-acho	...	*Zomalizo*
O bu onye k'anyi na-acho	...	*Zomalizo*
E Nweke k'anyi na-acho	...	*Zomalizo*
O chube iyi	...	*Zomalizo*
Ya lata o	...	*Zomalizo*
O jebe Olu-o	...	*Zomalizo*
Ya lata-o	...	*Zomalizo*
O jebe ahia o	...	*Zomalizo*
Ya lata o	...	*Zomalizo*

---

[12] Ruth Finnegan, *Oral Poetry*, London, Cambridge University Press, 1977, p.8

O bu onye?	...	*Zomalizo*
Nweke k'anyi na-acho	...	*Zomalizo*[13]
Who do we seek?	...	Zomalizo
Who do we seek?	...	Zomalizo
It's Nweke that we seek	...	Zomalizo
When he goes to the stream	...	Zomalizo
May he return	...	Zomalizo
When he goes to work	...	Zomalizo
May he return	...	Zomalizo
When he goes to the market	...	Zomalizo
May he return	...	Zomalizo
Who do we seek?	...	Zomalizo
It is Nweke that we seek	...	Zomalizo

(Translation by the author)

As the mourners, led by the singer, conduct their 'search,' variations of the song are introduced in the same breath. The deceased had previously (in a symbolic sense) traversed many lands and returned, but this journey suggests a final, irrevocable parting. With the end of the search comes the reconciliation to the fact that the person has truly 'gone.' Chinua Achebe's adapts this death song in his own poem '*Uno Onwu Okigbo*' as will be shown in the later chapter.

---

[13] F.C. Ogbalu, *Abu Igbo*, Onitsha, Merit Standard Press, 1974, p. 184

Journey

Tied to the search, the motif of journey recurs frequently in the African dirge song. Most often this is insinuated in the idea that the dead person has gone on a long journey, and his return is being awaited. In *'Onuma'* for instance, this journey motif is realised in the last line as a rhetorical question: 'I am asking, where has my sister gone?'

In *'Onye Nzoputa,'* we see this journey motif once again being asserted as an excuse for the absence of the deceased at the gathering of her fellow women. The poet-mourner says:

> Somebody please play the Ozirigbo
> Let me see if she will come (to life)

The musical instrument (Ozirigbo) becomes an object of invocation that summons the departed back to the land of the living. The motif intensifies the idea of final separation, dissolution, disconnection or detachment of the deceased from the affairs of the living.

Also noticeable in *'When Death comes to fetch you'* is a similar journey motif. Pagak, the land of the ancestors, is a destination, a locale that mother death leads her children. All must make that journey when the time comes. Every medicine is effective and could cure any disease as long as it is not yet time for the person to embark on the last journey to

'Pagak.' Once the time comes, nothing can hold him back from 'travelling' to the land of the dead. With this understanding comes a realisation of the role of death as a messenger who helps in that mythic transportation from the land of living to that of the dead.

Perhaps this idea of journey explains the elaborate preparations that accompany some funeral rites in parts of Africa. A chief is buried with his retinue of slaves and servants, including a few household items. These slaves and servants go with him to help carry his belongings to the land of the dead, and of course, also help him settle there. A woman is normally buried with her cooking utensils, best wrappers and blouses, and sometimes new dresses presented to the deceased by the mourners. All these are included to enable her 'travel' well and settle down quickly in her new place of abode.

The African dirge structure

African dirge poems celebrate death. The varying structures of composition suggest the distinctive elements of African dirge poetry. Ruth Finnegan notes four different types of African oral dirges based on their structure of composition. These she classified as types 'A,' 'B,' 'C,' and 'D.'[14] However the four types have been incorporated into

---

[14] Ruth Finnegan, *Oral Literature in Africa*, Nairobi, Oxford University Press, 1970, p.158

two broad categories identified here. They are the *solo* and *choral* dirges. The term 'broad' implies that there is no clear-cut distinction between both types as features of one may often recur in the other. The major difference, as examples reveal, lies in their structural representations: while the solo dirges are usually lengthy with a preponderance of heavy rhythm and mood, the popular tunes are often short, with a line or two lyrical notes.

Solo Dirges

These are dirges specially composed for a specific instance and relayed in 'new' rhythms. Such poems are inspired by instances of death or other tragedies and are normally composed for the dead person. The poems are 'new' in the sense that their lyrics and rhythms have not been used prior to the time of delivery.

These dirges are overshadowed by a preponderance of emotions that are evoked and sustained by enumerating the sterling qualities of the dead. Sometimes the name of the dead is mentioned, including a delineation of his family tree. Sometimes too, the cause of death is hinted. Often the rendition is realised with a proliferation of praise names and titles for the dead hero.

The Abigbo solo group is credited with the following

Igbo rendition:

Echeta Uwa araa ogwu,
Nwoke Oma m ga akwara onye uwa?
Agam akwara onye uwa? Chi ejiele
Nwanyi emere eze mee nwa ya
A hunam uwa
A nene Lolo ogara ole ebe?
Nne le, onwu amaghi izu egbu o.
Onwu amaghi izu egbu o
Gini mere ome ihe oma ji anwu ngwa ngwa?
Okele la aba ogu onye nwem ni
Aga ana nju mere ihe okwu
Onwu emebiele anyi obi la eziokwu
Dede Maurice eh
Ogara anyi otu otu owu eziokwu
Ajugham nwunem nwanyi ogara ele ebe?[15]

When you think of hardship you take drugs
Good friends to whom shall I speak
Of my sorrow?
To whom shall I tell my sorrows?
Darkness has come upon me
Woman that was made a queen,
Whose children were made royal
The world is hard on me
Lolo first born of my sisters,

Where has she gone?

Mother, death kills thoughtlessly

---

[15] R. N Egudu and D.I Nwoga ed., 1973, p. 72

> Death kills without regard
> Why does she who does good die too early?
> Son of my sister, great warrior,
> Owner of my person
> He who listens as he walks has given cause for trouble
> Truly, death has injured our hearts
> Maurice, elder brother
> Truly we each have a share in death
> I am asking where has my sister gone?
> (Translated by Egudu and Nwoga)

The tragic sense of loss is captured in repeated rhetorical questions:

> *Nwoko oma mga akwara onye uwa?*
> *A gam akwara onye uwa?*
>
> To whom shall I speak of my sorrows?
> To whom shall I tell my sorrows?

Death is dressed in vestiges of 'darkness' and 'hardship' (Line 4). This tragic sense is further heightened by the enduring nobility and royal background of the deceased (lines 5-8). Soon, the poet turns philosophical, pondering on death and ironies of fate (lines 9-11).

The effects of this dirge range from states of

bitterness, acute pain and frustration. Overall, there emerges a deeply philosophical understanding of death. In '*Onuma,*' each line of utterance may hide philosophical themes behind the literal meaning.

> *Gini mere ome ihe oma ji anwu ngwa ngwa?*
> *Onwu emebiele anyi obi ne eziokwu*
> *Dede Maurice eh*
> *O gara anyi otu otu owu eziokwu*

> Why does she who does good die too early?
> Truly Death had injured our hearts
> Maurice elder brother
> Truly we all have a share in Death.

Here, the mourner contemplates fate and other such ironies of human misfortune. An Igbo proverb says 'those whom the gods love are called home early.' Such juxtaposition of good and evil in the circumstance of attendant fate is suggestive not merely of heroic destiny but importantly also the inevitably common decimal of sorrow and love in all human experience. It is paradoxical that the 'noble heart' often meets an untimely death. This paradox of good and evil is compulsive of the heroic destiny and points to the inevitability of sorrow and loss in profound human experience (Line 13).

In contrast, *'Onye Nzoputa'* which mourns the matron of a female dance group takes on the character of praise, tilting toward a colourful ululation for the dead.

Ogatu onye ona ara ahu nnem le
Ama mmiri ako ncha, nne le
Ulo shopu m na ekome akwa, nnem le
Ibara di na nwanyi, nnem le
Ulo oma m na eji eche aku, nnem le
Nne ukwu umu azi, nnem le
Oghu na ite nga, nnem le
Ihuna si ndomi ibe gi afutala
Ozirigbo ejiri chie ya eze
Majuo ma ha onokwa ya
Unu kutu ozirigbo mele ye ma ona abia

Saviour of those in difficulty, mother
Road to the stream never without soap, mother
Shop where cloths are displayed, mother
Joy of the married state, mother
Beautiful house where wealth is preserved, mother
Ozirigbo used in your enthroning
Is it still there I ask?
Somebody please play the Ozirigbo
Let me see if she will come.
(Translated by Egudu and Nwoga)

Copious descriptive epithets are deployed to

highlight a gentle, generous and loving personality. Her loss, seen in this light becomes a tragic one indeed. The repetition of 'mother' achieves a heightening of pathos. It is an invocation of the spirit of the departed, capturing the agony of the mourner.

More important still is the motif of search which recurs in the last line of the first stanza.

> *Unu kutu Ozirigbo*
> *mele ma ya onokwa abia*
>
> Somebody please play the *Ozirigbo*
> Let me see if she will come (to life).

The 'ozirigbo' is played in accompaniment. The dead is normally sought in familiar environs as had earlier been stated. In this instance, it is her professional team who searches for her through the dance and song performance. So in this poem, the search is artistic rather than literal. It is also spiritual, borne from divine longing and nostalgia. Dramatisation of the search can only vary from one funeral tradition to another. In the second stanza,

> *Isi ingini na ehe ala nnem ukwu*
> *Ndomi ibe gi na akwa akwa*
> *A taa ga wu otu afo kamgbe anyi*
> *Choghe-ga gi*

Anyi acho chaala ya, anyi ahughi ya
Ogatu onye ona ara ahu, anyi ahughi ya
Unu kuirim recordu m ele ye ma oga abia
Ezi okwu anyi ele ye ma ona abia le
Anyi egwucha recordu anyi ahughi ya
Anyi ahughi nne
Ihuna si ura kwere izu aghola onwu

Engine head that shakes the earth, my big mother
Today fellow women are mourning
Today is a year since we have searched for you
We have searched and have not found her
We haven't seen her, mother, saviour of those in difficulty
Please start our dance
Let us see whether she will come
Truly let us see whether she is coming
We finished playing our dance and did not see her
Don't you see, sleep that lasts a week has become death.
(Translated by Egudu and Nwoga)

Mourning continues with lavish epithets in praise of the deceased:

Isi ingini na he ala, nnem ukwu

(Engine head that shakes the earth, my big mother)

This iconic engine-head is intended to depict the

power and influence of the heroine even at death. Her presence, wherever she went, could not but 'shake the earth.' The range of imagery available to the mourner is unlimited in time and space. Modern and traditional activities like 'engine,' 'shop' and traditional '*ozirigbo*' are in constant poetic exchange. This fusion of traditional and modern affirms the necessity of both elements in present-day African expressions.

Choral Dirges

The second category is tagged the 'choral.' These are normally short and catchy songs rendered in groups. The rhythms are familiar although the lyrics may differ. Finnegan had rightly observed that in most African traditional performances,

> even with a familiar song there is room for variations on words or tune in actual delivery so that each performance in a sense may be a 'new' song[16]

In line with the tradition of popular dirges which mostly involves poet-audience interaction, we have such poems like 'Anyi-na-acho' and 'Iwe.'

---

[16] Ruth Finnegan, 1970, p. 267

(a)

Anyi na acho, cho cho

Anyi na-acho
Anyi na-acho nwanne anyi furu kamgbe echi-o
Anyi na-acho nwanne anyi furu kamgbe echi-o
Onye obuna choba-o
K'anyi mara ebe o no o
Choba ya[17]

We are searching, searching
We are searching
We are searching for our sister
Gone since yesterday
We are searching for our sister
Gone since yesterday
Everyone help and search
That we may know where she's gone
Everyone search for her

(b)

Anyi ga-ewere ya iwe?
K'anyi ga-abara ya mba?
K'anyi ga etinye aka n'obi
Tie Onwu! Chei Onwu!

Anyi ga-ewere ya iwe?
K'anyi ga-akwara ya akwa?

---

[17] Arondizuogo Chant recorded during a funral ceremony at Ndiuche, Arondizuogu in 1990. Translated by the author

K'anyi ga etinye aka n'obi
Tie Onwu! Chei Onwu![18]

Shall we be angry?
Or shall we rebuke it?
Or shall we beat our chest
and cry Death! O Death!

Shall we be angry?
Or shall we weep?
Or shall we beat our chest
And cry Death! O Death!

'*Anyi-na-acho*' Poem (a) and '*Iwe*' Poem (b) carry a mixture of light and comic, as well as sad and sombre, emotions. Both poems project the philosophical acceptance of that which is inevitable as well as irremediable. 'Iwe' does not simply express helplessness and mystification, it carries the philosophy of non-resistance and self surrender.

On the contrary, '*Onye Ije Lawa*' resonates like a farewell song to the soul of a departed one:

Onye Ije lawa uwa
Iyo! Iyoo! Iyo!
Odika bewe akwa
Iyo! Iyoo! Iyo!

---

[18] Aba Traditional Chant rendered during a burial ceremony at Aba in 1991. Translated by the author

> When a traveller leaves the world
> Iyo! Iyoo! Iyo!
> We would want to cry
> Iyo! Iyoo! Iyo!

The leader chants to the response of the chorus who imitates the sound of wailing in the background. The body may be at the point of being intered and mourning takes a sharp burst in the final lines *'Cha-a! ho! ho!,'* the succeeding in the last line *'Cha-a he! he! he!'* achieving the effect of phoneaesthetic variation.

> *Umuna liwe ya*
> *Iyo! Iyoo! Iyo!*
> *Onuma eju ha obi*
> *Iyo! Iyoo! Iyo!*
> *Cha-a! ho! Ho! Ho!*
> *Cha-a ho!*
> *Ho! Ho!*[19]

> When his brethren are burying him
> Iyo! Iyoo! Iyo!
> Sorrow fills their hearts
> Iyo! Iyoo! Iyo!
> Cha-a! ho! Ho! Ho!
>
> Cha-a he! He! He!

The light-hearted mood that permeates this dirge is

---

[19] F. C. Ogbalu, 1974, p. 179. Translated by the author

achieved by adopting an attitude of poetic objectivity or distancing while treating the tragic theme. This is further communicated by the lead-singer, using the third person, in addressing the deceased and the mourners:

> '*Onye Ije*' (traveller) instead of the name of the dead.
> '*Umunna*' (brethren) instead of '*anyi*' (we).
> '*ha*' (them) instead of '*anyi*' (us).

The view of man's tragic destiny is realised in this dirge by the appropriate use of the term '*Onye Ije*' in addressing the departed.

Language of African dirge

The language of dirge poetry is usually full of emotive solicitations. In giving expression to the tragic memory brought about by death, the poet resorts to creating mental pictures as a way of communicating the deep loss and apparent injustice meted by death.

There are two discernible positive and negative emotive reactions in most African dirge poems. While the deceased, his relatives, including the mourner, are fondly remembered with doting phrases, death and company are cast in pejorative associations. In expressing the negative sentiments in the Ugandan poem *'If Death were not there,'* the revulsion which death induces is alluded in extension to the inheritor. Hence the juxtaposition of 'death' with the 'inheritor' becomes a kind of insult or satire.

> This inheritor is most lucky;
> Ee, brother tell me,
> If death were not there,
> Ugly one, whose daughter would have married you?

The contemporary nature of some of the images and epithets used within the oral mode of poetic expression attests to an interdependence of both poetic expressions in present dirge traditions. *'Onye Nzoputa'* for instance is realised with profuse modernities although it is essentially an oral poem. The deft deployment of images is realised in several ways, a few which are discussed here:

Personifications

Personifications predominate the literary features of the African dirge. In *'When Death comes to fetch You,'* death is presented as a benevolent mother who entices children with sweet things like 'simsim' paste and 'white ants' paste/mixed with shea-butter.' Her children are always 'obedient,/loyal' and they 'jump up gladly,' 'without brushing the dust' off their buttocks, just to answer her call. At other instances like in *'The Beautiful Playground'* death is featured as a very wicked king who goes about slaying people without reprieve.

Metaphors and Similes

In *'Onuma'* death is a metaphor for pain, separation and disillusionment, involving not only the mourner, but also his relations 'Maurice elder brother.'

'Onwu abua m k'ede' (death uproots me like cocoyam) used in *'Ikwa Uwa'* helps in expressing the sense of abandonment and helplessness that the persona feels at the departure of the relative.

Hyperboles

This often occurs as exaggeration of the feelings of loss, damage, or loneliness brought about by death. In *'Ikwa uwa'* the persona at a time exclaims that death has '... turned me into bitterness itself.' This statement is hyperbolic in the literal sense (the impossibility of becoming 'bitterness itself'). But what is achieved is a total feeling of desolation, gloom, bleakness and devastation which is the poet's intention or actual condition.

Apostrophes

Sometimes there is a direct address to the deceased. In this poem for example, we have the following lines of admonition:

Naa nti n'ihem na-ekwu
Uwa gi ozo
Nne gi gwa gi okwu
Nuo-o!
Nna gi gwa gi okwu
Nuo-o!
Nwanne gi gwa gi okwu
Nuo-o!
Enyi gi gwa gi okwu
Nuo-o!
Akpochile nti-o
Akpochile obi-o
N' anughi anu-o
N' anu n'ili-o![20]

Listen to what I say
In your next life
Listen! When mother talks (to you)
Listen! When father talks (to you)
Listen! When brother talks (to you)
Listen! When friends talk (to you)
Do not close you ears
Do not harden your heart
For the deaf-to-word
Will surely hear in the grave!

The above lament features a stubborn teenager who

---

[20] A burial ceremony: Orlu, Imo State, 1999. Recording and translation by the author.

met death through questionable circumstances. He is advised to heed the mistakes of the past and take definite corrective measures in another incarnation. What is most interesting in this direct address to the deceased is the re-affirmation of the inter-relatedness of the spiritual world with corporeal reality. Africans usually speak of the soul of the departed as if the world of the living and dead were realities that are demarcated only by a veil of invisibility.

Invocations

Other times this awareness on the part of the poet-mourner, of the co-existence of the physical and supernatural worlds, is expressed more forcefully in the form of an invocation. Invocation therefore becomes a poetic feature in African dirge. This is realised through constantly repeated invitations to the departed soul of the deceased to 'come down' and accomplish immediate actions either in the spirit world, or in the physical world. In *'Onye Nzoputa'* the repetitions of the phrase 'nnem-le' (my mother-o) and 'mother!' in *'Lament for Bala'nku'* raise the repetitive chant to that of an invocation.

Repetitions

Repetition of phrases, names and ideas is quite common in the African dirge. Sometimes where phrases are repeated as in *'Akwa Udu'* (Lament),

> *Agara si n'onwu gbara ikpo*
> *Agara si n'onwu gbara ikpo*
> *Agara si n'onwu gbara ikpo* [21]

it is for tonal variation in the aesthetics of performance which enjoins deeper appreciation of the feelings being expressed. At other times, like in this excerpt from Vandau poem from Mozambique, we have the refrain coming up in different stanzas of the poem:

> *Where shall I find one*
> *Like to Bala'nku,*
> *Mother!*
> *Like to Bala'nku,*
> *Mother!*
>
> *Where shall I find one*
> *Like to Bala'nku,*
>
> *Mother!*
>
> *Like to Bala'nku,*
>
> *Mother!*
>
> *Mother, Mother, Mother,*
> *Ma-mai-ne,*
> *Like to Bala'nku*
>
> *He brought me unto goodly things*
> *All these I did possess*
> *He showed me joy*
>
> *Mother!*

---

[21] Recording and translation by the author, from the Masquerade dance, Arondizuogu: 1992.

> *None like Bala'nku*
> *Mother, mother, mother*
> *Ma-mai-ne*
> *Mother!*
> *None like Bala'nku*[22]

The line repetitions:

> *Like to Bala'nku,*
> *Mother!*

serve as chorus for each stanza of the poem. The repetition also helps in sustaining the grief and sense of loss heightened by the cry *'ma-mai-ne,'* in subsequent stanzas.

'Akwa Udu' (Lament), probably more than any other testifies to the panegyric nature of the African dirge.

> *Agara si n'onwu gbara ikpo*
> *Agara si n'onwu gbara ikpo*
> *Agara si n'onwu gbara ikpo*
> *Anyi aka ama mgbe onwu na-eji abia nu-o*
> *Were zonahu-nu ya Udu be anyi-o*
> *Obere ahia na-ehi udu Nkwo Fada*
> *Odi-na-mba mba na-akara akwa-o*
> *Odi-na-mba mba na-akara akwa-o*
> *Odi-na-mba mba na-akara akwa-o*
> *Ejem ta ebe nnunu mmuo-o*[23]

---

[22] Chinweizu, 1988, p. 311

[23] Rendition by the Masquerade dance group, Arondizuogu: 1992. Translation by the author

If only Death could wear a bell
If only Death could wear a bell
If only Death could wear a bell
Then we would have known when it comes
Then we would have hidden Udu my brother
Diminutive Udu of Nkwo Fada
Stranger mourned even in other lands
Stranger mourned even in other lands
Stranger mourned even in other lands
Shall I cry louder than the night owl.

The dead is praised (lines 6-9). Udu's (deceased) fame is comparable to the big and popular *Nkwo Fada* market of the community (line 6). The praise name of '*Odina-mba mba na-akwara akwa*' (repeated twice) glorifies the departed and takes on the likeness of an apotheosis.

Chapter 3

Igbo Written Traditions

'Uno Onwu Okigbo' * *'Okigbo Ebelebe Egbuele'*
* *'Odogwu Kabral'*

The distinguished African scholar and literary critic, Donatus Nwoga, discusses the mentality and mode of traditional, as opposed to modern, contexts of African aesthetics. 'Our concept of traditional,' he says, 'which has its antithesis 'modern' are both separated in the African context, not so much by time as by mentality and mode.

'This mode of distinction,' he goes on to say, 'is whether the verse belongs to the written tradition or to the oral tradition.'[1]

It serves to explain what some Igbo writers have done which is to adapt popular renditions and attribute them to definite history and persons. One of the best examples of this adaptation and localisation is the poem '*Uno onwu Okigbo*' by Chinua Achebe.

---

[1] D. I. Nwoga ed., *Perspectives on Okigbo*, Washington DC, Three Continents Press, 1984, Introduction

'Uno Onwu Okigbo'

Here, the poet-mourner is not just a borrower from tradition; he attempts to perpetuate tradition by employing a popular death song of the community:

Obu onye k'anyi n'acho?	Who do we seek?
Obu onye k'anyi na-acho?	Who do we seek?
Okigbo k'anyi n'acho	It's Okigbo we seek
Nzomalizo	Nzomalizo
Ojebe nku, nya nata	When he goes to fetch wood
Ochu b'iyi, nya nata	May he return
Ojebe afia, nya nata	When he goes to stream
Okigbo k'ayi n'acho	May he return
Nzomalizo	When he goes to the market
	May he come back
Obu onye k'ayi n'acho?	It's Okigbo we seek
Obu ?nye k'ayi n'acho?	Nzomalizo
Okigbo k'ayi n'acho	
Nzomalizo	...
Ojebe nku, ugboko elikwunia	May work never swallow him
Ochu b'iyi, iyi elikwania	May he never drown in the water
Ojebe afia, Uzu afia elikwania	May he not be devoured by the market
Ojebe agha, ogbunigwe doo	At war, greetings to his comrade
Okigbo k'ayi n'acho	It's Okigbo that we seek
Nzomalizo	Nzomalizo
Ezite egwu Onye g'achi?	Who will rally at the playground
Eseta Ogu Onye g'agba	Who will fight the war
Okigbo k'ayi n'acho	It's Okigbo that we seek

Nzomalizo	Nzomalizo
Nee egwu k'Onabia	See! the dance is coming
Nee Ogu n'odaa	See! war is approaching
Ogu egwu choo	The dance of war
Dike Ogu chaa	The warrior has come
Okigbo k'ayi n'acho	It's Okigbo that we seek
Nzomalizo	Nzomalizo
	The dance is done
Egwu anaa!	My drummer
Oti-igba muo!	My own brother
Okolo nnem!	Son of Igboland
Okolo Igbo!	When a youth confronts his mate (and)
Okolobia n'ogbo mmee	Gallantry has gone to the dead
Ogalanya na be mmuo	It's Okigbo that we seek
Okigbo k'ayi n'acho	
Nzomalizo[2]	(*Translation by the author*)

In the traditional poem '*Onye k'anyi na-acho*,' the deceased, Nweke symbolises Everyman who has finally gone the way of his ancestors. Thus the search for the deceased becomes central in the performance:

O bu onye k'anyi na-acho .... *Zomalizo*
O bu onye k'anyi na-acho .... *Zomalizo*
E Nweke k'anyi na-acho .... *Zomalizo*

---

[2] Chinua Achebe and Dubem Okafor [Ed.] *Don't Let Him Die: An anthology of Memorial Poems for Christopher Okigbo 1932-67* Enugu: Fourth Dimension Publishers, 1978 p. 53

Who do we seek? .... Zomalizo
Who do we seek .... Zomalizo
It's Nweke that we seek .... Zomalizo

Achebe however lends identity to Everyman. Christopher Okigbo, in his improvisation, is the man.

> *Obu onye k'anyi n'acho?*
> *Obu onye k'anyi na-acho?*
> *Okigbo k'anyi n'acho*

> Who do we seek?
> Who do we seek?
> It's Okigbo we seek

The search is for Okigbo, as in the traditional version, is paramount for the poet in so much as it is constantly set against the motif of departure with recurring rhetorical questions:

'Obu onye...' (Who is it...?)

Both poems convey traditional *ideas* of journey associated with death *olu/ugbo* (work); *iyi* (stream); *ahia/afia* (market); and the poetic supplication to the departed hero to come back among his people. The supplication is fervent by its recurrence via the proliferation of the device of lexical parallelisms: *'ya la ta-o'* punctuated with the chorus of *'Zomalizo.'* The poet further extends the images of death to incorporate that of modern warfare,

> *Ojebe agha ogbonuke doo*
> (At war the hero of his comrades)

Even without any direct mention of the Biafran war with Nigeria, the poet succeeds in creating the tension and expectations of war. This is achieved by repeated echoes of shooting and violence;

> *Nee egwu k'onabia*
> *Nee ogu n'odaa*
> *Ogu-egwu choo*
> *Dike ogu chaa...*
> *Okolobia n'ogbo mmee*
> *Ogalanya na be mmoo*
>
> See! Dance is coming
> See! War is coming
> The dance of war
> The warrior has come...
> When the youth confronts his mate (and)
> Gallantry has gone to the dead's land

Okigbo, victim of the war, is mourned for the loss of a rich and versatile talent. His departure is symbolised as the end of the dance and the death of the drummer;

> *Egwu annaa!*
> *Oti-igba muo*
> *Okolo nnem*
> *Okolo Igbo*

> The dance is done
> My drummer
> My own brother
> Son of Igboland

The deceased hero is equally dressed in communal epithets.

> *Okolo nnem* (my own mother's son),
>
> *Okolo Igbo* (great son of Igboland).

He is the virile young man who met his match when gallantry goes to its death.

Even with Achebe's 'Onitsha-Igbo' dialectal variant in *'Uno Onwu Okigbo,'* ('*afia*' for '*ahia*' (market), '*ugbo*' for '*oru*' (work), the use of the prefix '*N*' of '*Nzomalizo*' for '*Zomalizo*,' and the use of '*k'ayi*' instead of '*k'anyi*,' and '*n'acho*') the adaptation is a more realised artistic individuation than its traditional precursor.

Thus Achebe's poem, which is simpler in content,

provides our framework of the dirge with the lead singer and the '*Zomalizo*' repetitive chorus coming in its wake. This structure evokes the funeral performance in traditional Igboland. Its adaptation in 'modern' dirge composition situates the poem fully in its distinct cultural milieu and richly portrays the dirge aesthetics of African literature.

'*Okigbo Ebelebe Egbuole*'

While Achebe exploits the funeral structure of Igbo dirge as a movement towards an African dirge aesthetics, the author of '*Okigbo Ebelebe Egbuole*' achieves something similar through his creative manipulation of Igbo tonal rhythms and images drawn from the communal flora and fauna.

Emeka Chimezie in rendering this composition in Nsukka[3] specifically demonstrated to his over four hundred audience that he was coming from a familiar cultural background. In his paper entitled 'Igbo War Poetry,' he avers that,

> the Igbo have what is generally
> regarded as the highest form of
> literature, or as the elevated

---

[3] University of Nigeria, Nsukka: Second International Seminar on Igbo literature in August 1981.

> expression of elevated thought or feeling in metrical form, meant for warfare.[4]

Chimezie further amplifies this view graphically:

> Those born and bred in Igboland or who long have trod on her sand and do her language understand will see the Igbo society as a hive of poesy where hardly any utterance escapes poetic romance with fighting, playing, working stanzaically punctuated and advice, warning, teaching poetically reconstructed[5]

The poet's handling of *'Ebelebe Egbuole'* is familiar within the context of traditional 'abu onwu agha' (war dirge) of the Igbo. 'Okigbo Ebelebe Egbuole' was his own poetic reconstruction of the dirge in honour of the hero who fell fighting in the battle for Biafran nationality.

'Okigbo Ebelebe Egbuole'

E nyem mkpisi akwukwo m'echeta Okigbo
E nyem mpempe akwukwo m'echeta Okigbo

---

[4] Emeka Chimezie, 'Igbo War Poetry', Second International Seminar on Igbo Literature held under the auspices of the Society for the Promotion of Igbo Language and Culture (SPILC) at the University of Nigeria, Nsukka, 12-15 August, 1981 p. 2

[5] Emeka Chimezie, 1981, p. 1

A si mu guwa edemede m'echeta Okigbo
Aluchaana m ogu lota na Nsukka aghughim Okigbo

Lee! Egbuole Okigbo!
Lee! Egbuole Okigbo-E!
Umuigbo lee! Egbuole Okigbo!
Ndi gburunu Okigbo, Okigbo o mere gini?
Ebelebe egbuole!

Chei! Professor Chinua Achebe lee egbuole Okigbo
Professor Obiechina lee, egbuole Okigbo!
Professor Nwoga, Professor Egudu,
Aru emenum-o
A hukwaghim Okigbo O jere ebee? Njiji ejiele

Cyprian Ekwensi lee, Egbuole Okigbo
Gabriel Okara, Wole Soyinka, J.P Clark Mo-o
Mazi Ogbalu, Nolue Emenanjo, Nnamdi Olebara lee
Gwam otu m ga-eme, olaedo efuole, ebelebe egbuole

Omeji puge epuge, ha elee ya gbajie, kwim!
Anyanwu chaga achaga chi ewere ehihie jie, gwiim!
Okuko bugara anyi akwa, ha elee ya zogbuo, piaa!
Ndi gburu Okigbo ejile ose saa mu ahu-o
Umuigbo, ahu afokwaghim-o

Agaara m buru egbe-eligwe, ndi gburu Okigbo
Mu agbagbusia ha, kwukwu-kwukwu-kwukwu
Kwa wara wara aaa!

Onye ejikwalam aka na ndi gburu
Okigbo aghukpolam anya
Onye abakwaralam mba ndi gburu Okigbo
Emena out
Ndi gburu Okigbo aruola ala puo eze elu
Okigbo ebelebe egbuole!

Professor Uche Okeke lee! Ndi gburu
Okigbo wu anya ahu iheoma
Dr. Philip Nwachukwu ndi gburu
Okigbo wu anya eso iheoma
Ugo chi nyere umu Igbo ha ewere ya gbue!
Ha ewere ya gbuo-o! Obi fere ha azu
Chukwu ekwekwala njo!

Agam asi ndi gburu ya mgbo…mgbo
…piawapukwa ha isi?
Umuagbara ndi isi isii, ndi isis asaa,
Chumakwala ha oso?
Amadioha, Ogwuiduekeazara, Igwekala
Chuba ha?
Ebili ukpabi chuba kugbuo ha?
Unu ejena Chukwu nwe ikpe!

Ejerem mmemme okochi, okochi Okigbo ako-e
Achebe echebe bebe bebenu Okigbo-e
Aniakor akoba akuko kotanu Okigbo-e
Anyamiri ekweghim-o
Lelenu Okigbo ebe o kwum n'ihu-o

Mmadu nu anu adogbuola Okigbo

Mmadu bu Ekwensu agbajala Okigbo e
Obasanjo na *My command*, I s'onye gburu Okigbo?
Onye gburu Okigbo-e, I ma ama ezo
Ajuju chere gi[6]

When I see a writing pen I remember Okigbo
When I see a piece of scroll I remember Okigbo
Ask me to read a speech I'll remember Okigbo
Back to Nsukka from the war, I cannot find Okigbo

Have you heard? They have killed Okigbo
Have you heard? They have killed Okigbo
Country men hear! Okigbo is dead!
Those who killed Okigbo, what did he do?
O disaster has befallen me!

Professor Chinua Achebe see, they
Have killed Okigbo
Professor Obiechina see, they've killed Okigbo
Professor Nwoga, Professor Egudu,
A horrible act is done!
I can't find Okigbo, where has he gone?
Darkness is fallen!

Cyprian Ekwensi see,
Okigbo has been killed
Gabriel Okara, Wole Soyinka, and my own J.P Clark
Mazi Ogbalu, 'Nolue Emenanjo,

---

[6] Emeka Chimezie, p. 18

Nnamdi Olebara see
What am I to do now? The gold is lost,
Disaster has struck!

The yam sapling has been nipped in the bud, gwim!
The shining sun is eclipsed by sudden
Darkness, gwiim!
The cock that crows for us has been
Crushed, piaa!
Murderers of Okigbo have rubbed pepper
On my face
O my people, I am finished

Shall I summon thunder to destroy these
Killers?
Don't hold me, killers of Okigbo have
Made me blind.
No one must rebuke me, killers of
Okigbo have done evil!
Killers of Okigbo have committed abomination!
Okigbo, disaster has fallen on me!

Professor Uche Okeke see, *the-eye-that
Spite-good-things* have killed Okigbo
Dr. Philip Nwachukwu, these killers are
Eyes-that-loath-good

The-golden-eagle has been killed
They seized and killed him, those
Heartless ones! O God forbid!

Shall I invoke thunder to strike them?
Or the six and seven headed spirits to
Chase them?
Amadioha, Ogwuodekeazara, Igwekala
Chase them?
Ebili Ukpabi pursue and smash them?
O-no! God alone will judge.

I went to the festival of the sun, but
The sun of Okigbo is set
Achebe in his thought, has cried for Okigbo
Aniakor has told tales and told about Okigbo
My tears overflow
See Okigbo standing before me

Beastly men have devoured Okigbo
Devilish men have shattered Okigbo
Obasanjo and *My Command*, you said
Who killed Okigbo?
You can hide now murderer, but judgement
Awaits you
(Translation by the author)

Of significance in the above dirge is not only the vision of the hero as a priceless gem and worthy patriot of immense talents, but the communal accord and agreement as to the stature of the hero. The names of equally famed sons of the land are copiously cited in the second and third stanzas of the poem.

These include the best of Africa's literary fleet: Chinua Achebe, Cyprian Ekwensi, Gabriel Okara, Wole Soyinka, Bekederemo Clark. There are also other celebrated intellectuals: Donatus Nwoga, Emmanuel Obiechina and Romanus Egudu, Mazi Ogbalu, 'Nolue Emenanjo, Nnamdi Olebara, some of whom participated at the international conference on Igbo literature where the poem was presented. This is no mere dramatic stereotype. It is an artistic device which is intended to mark or emphasise value: i.e., the true worth of the hero among his peers (or age-grades in Igbo tradition):

> *Professor Chinua Achebe lee*
> *Egbuele Okigbo-o*
> *Professor Obiechina lee*
> *Egbuele Okigbo-ee*
> *Professor Nwoga, Professor Egudu*
> *Aru emenum-o, a hukwaghim Okigbo*
> *O jere ebee, njiji ejiela*
>
> Professor Chinua Achebe
> They have killed Okigbo

> Professor Obiechina, see
> They have killed Okigbo
> Professor Nwoga, Professor Egudu
> Tragedy has befallen me.
> I cannot find Okigbo, where has he gone?
> Darkness has befallen me!

While the poetry thus achieves the high point of traditional poetry in the common celebration of a communal essence, the fourth stanza marks a change in the movement and focuses on the hero, memories of whom are laden with 'wreaths' of epithets depicting his untimely death. He is the 'yam bud broken before its bloom; the sun shut out all of a sudden by a jealous eclipse; the cock that crows beautifully at dawn, trampled to death by enemies.' The killers of Okigbo have inflicted a most painful torture on the poet and all of us. They have 'scrubbed our eyes with pepper,' which means inflicted a terrible pain.

> *Omeji puga epuga, ha elee ya gbajie, gwim!*
> *Anyanwu chaga achaga, chi ewere*
> *Ehihie jie, gwiim!*
> *Okuko bugara anyi akwa, ha elle*
> *Ya zogbuo, piaa!*
> *Ndi gburu Okigbo ejile ose saa mu*
> *Ahu-o*
> *Umuigbo, ahu afokwaghim-o-o!*

> The yam sapling has been nipped
> In the bud
> The sun is eclipsed by
> Sudden darkness
> The cock that crows for us has
> Been crushed!
> Okigbo's killers have rubbed pepper
> In my face
> O! my people, I am finished!

We are taken to the contemplation of vengeance (Line 25). What action against the malefactors may be fitting? Killing them by invocation of supernatural forces (thunder, lightning)? Such imagined reprisals could only be commensurate with the crime of cutting short the life of a prodigious talent --as if prodigy mattered in the senseless violence and bloodshed of battlefields.

> *Ndi gburu Okigbo emene otu!*
> *Ndi gburu Okigbo aruoala puo eze elu-oo*
>
> Killers of Okigbo have done evil
> Killers of Okigbo have committed abomination!

The killers are the typical killjoy in a most vile sense; they have a heart of stone (stanza 7).

> *...ndi gburu Okigbo bu anya ahu iheoma*

...obi fere ha azu

...these killers are eyes-that-loath-good
...they are heartless one!

This emotional indignation which is but an artistic extension of war sentiment progresses into subsequent stanzas with the regular question: what retribution can be visited on the enemy? The options are many. Rhetorically presented: death to the enemies by gunfire, bullets to shatter their heads, six-headed and seven-headed spirits to haunt them for the rest of their lives? Other supernaturalistic options include: Amadioha (god of thunder), Igwekala (god of the skies), Ogwudekeazara and Ebili Ukpabi (great gods of Iboland) to track them down and slay them? Unfortunately, the poet appears to relent. He solicits, in their stead, some form of divine arbitration in an almost anti-climatic suspension of action: To God belongs the judgement. By choosing so, the poet has invoked the Igbo *ofo*, which one of Igbo scholar explicates as

Oka-ikpe gburu gburu uwa
Na-ekpe mmadu nile ikpe[7]
(symbol of the god
of justice)

---

[7] David Nwala, in an interview with the author, Aba Nigeria 1990.

The eighth and ninth stanzas are cast in wry humour using elements of pun and satire.

> *Ejerem mmemme Okochi, okochi Okigbo*
> *Ako-e*
> *Achebe che bebe bebenu Okigbo-e*
> *Aniakor akoba akuko, kotanu Okigbo-e*

> I went to the festival of the sun,
> But the sun of Okigbo is set
> Achebe in his thought has cried for Okigbo
> Aniakor has told tales and told about
> Okigbo

In the rhetoric of Igbo poetry, intonation is often manipulated for effects of variation, alliteration or pun. A cursory exploration of the pun, which is hinged upon the tonal nature of Igbo words and suffixes, shows the following discoveries:

Mmemme Okochi......................(literally, Sun festival)
Okochi Okigbo...................................(Okigbo's Sun)
Ako...(set)
Achebe...(sympathiser)
Echebe bebe................(pondered and wailed for Okigbo)
Aniakor..(sympathiser)
Akoba..(tells)
Akuko kotanu...........................(tales of about Okigbo)

The three-syllable word pattern and the low/ rising tone are maintained graphically in the stanza:

> A-che-be e-che-be...be-be-nu O-ki-gbo
> ...
> A-nia-kór a-kó-ba a-ku-kó kó-ta-nu- O-ki-gbo

This establishes a rhythmic (rising and falling) tonal structure for which the Igbo language is noted. More sound effects are produced by proliferating Igbo vowels /o/,/ó/,/a/,/e/ and the consonants /b/ and /k/. When these are sustained repeatedly throughout the stanza, the result is not only a spontaneous melody, but also a simulation of weeping.

> Achebe echebe bebe bebenu
> ...
> Okóchi ókóchi Okigbo ako-ee

The alliteration of /k/ is equally acoustically effective:

> Aniakór akóba akukó kótanu Okigbo

Furthermore, the suffix (*nu*) which also functions as modifier is employed here for stylistic 'highlighting':

> 'bebe<u>nu</u>' 'kóta<u>nu</u>'

This 'highlighting' extends the literal meaning of 'bebe' (cry) to wailing, and a'kóta' (to tell), to mourning or wailing. Yet in this surge of virtuosity, the poet manages to sustain the serious theme of loss. We are presently reminded of our lachrymal sensitivity. The poetic imagination is essential in African story-telling proficiency and this conjuration of the deceased is neither far-fetched nor surprising. We are told that tears overwhelm the poet as he sees the vision of Okigbo in front of him.

> *Anya mmiri ekweghim-o!*
> *Lelenu Okigbo ebe o kwum n'ihu-o!*

> My tears overflow
> I see Okigbo standing before me.

Further lamentations on the wickedness of human nature follow, satirising key persons involved in the hero's death. Man is a beast (that tears apart his kind). He is the devil (that seeks to destroy humanity).

> *Mmadu bu anu adogbuole Okigbo*
> *Mmadu bu Ekwensu agbajala Okigbo*
> *Obasanjo na My Command I s'onye*
> *Gburu Okigbo?*

Beastly men (have) devoured Okigbo
Devilish men (have) shattered Okigbo
Obasanjo and *My Command,*[8]
Who killed Okigbo?

This third line achieves double dramatic effects. It satirises history. As Barbara Thiering rightly states, 'historical study is admittedly always profoundly affected by one's own experience,'[9] Olusegun Obasanjo's war story beside his grandstanding, as far as the poet is concerned, fails to illuminate history. The rhetorical question to the author of *My Command* is also in the form of an accusation which places the addressee on the side of villains in the hero-villain divide of the Biafra-Nigeria war. The last line of the poem rests the case of who killed Okigbo. The murderer can hide but he cannot hide on judgement day –an interpolation of Christian religious belief in a day of judgement which, in a manner of speaking, coincides, only in part, with the Igbo tradition that some mysteries of fact are ultimately given up to arbitration by the gods.

Onye gburu Okigbo ee

---

[8] An autobiographical account of the Nigerian civil war by Olusegun Obasanjo who fought on the Nigerian side and received the instrument of surrrender from the Biafran army in 1970 .

[9] Barbara Thiering, *Jesus the Man*, Corgi, Britain, 1998 (Introduction.)

Ima ama ezo, ajuju chere gi

You can hide now murderer
But judgement awaits you

A dialectical divide of hero-victim and villain appears in this Igbo dirge. Death and its instruments which also include the killers of Okigbo are the villains. To mourn Okigbo, the hero-victim, the mourner surrounds himself with a host of sympathisers. On the side of the hero is the poet-mourner with a flock of sympathisers who have been noted earlier: Chinua Achebe, Obiechina, Nwoga, Egudu, Ekwensi, Okara, Emenanjo, Olebara, Okeke, Aniakor, etc, on the side of the villain is '*Onwu*' (Death), with images of destruction, *anu* (beast), *Ekwensu* (Devil), etc.

The overall purpose while still seeming to cast indictments on persons for their roles in the civil war also achieves the fuller realisation of the dirge sentiment: the final consolation through the expurgation of emotion.

Eee egbuole Okigbo
Eee egbuole Okigbo
Umuigbo lee egbuole Okigbo
Ndi gburunu Okigbo, omere gini?
Ebelebe egbuole!

They have killed Okigbo

They have killed Okigbo
Country men hear, Okigbo is dead
O killers, what was his crime?
O disaster has fallen!

During performance Chimezie's art comes out with greater clarity, eliciting spontaneous audience participation. On-the-spot declamation of sympathisers may enlarge to reflect the presence of other participants. Care is taken that the chorus is not given to idle repetitions. Noises of '*Chei*!! *Ei*! *Ei*!' are heard in the background. It is a participatory chant to enhance the sense of agony.

Chimezie's Igbo poetry is rich in a wide range of Igbo onomatopoeia, ideophones and phonoaesthetics.

Njinji ejiele...................darkness has fallen (disaster)
Ebelebe egbuole.............literally, tragedy has struck
Kwim!........................sound of something breaking
Gwiim!.......................simulation of falling object
Piaa!.........................simulation of crushing
Kwu Kwu Kwuuuu...........simulation of thunder

The historical sense of the poem as a narrative is a significant element in Igbo lamentation that cannot be overlooked. The mourner often traces the history of the deceased and circumstance involved in his death. In this case he is a veteran of war who only comes back to discover he has lost a dear friend.

> *Aluchaanam ogu lota na Nsukka*
> *Aghughim Okigbo*

> Back to Nsukka from the war
> I cannot find Okigbo

This marks the beginning of the search motif in Igbo dirge such as: Where has the dead gone to? What was (the nature of) his crime? The rhetorical questions are crucial to the motif of search and establishing the innocence of the victim.

> *Okigbo o jere ebee?...*
> *Okigbo o mere gini?...*
> *Onye gburu Okigbo?...*

> Where has Okigbo gone?...
> What has Okigbo done?...
> Who killed Okigbo?...

This traditional rendition becomes in addition a dramatic poem filled with exaggerated emotions and a high appeal to the dramatic.

Emeka Chimezie therefore is the communal mourner, using his primary language and the popular mode of rendition which involves the interaction between singer and audience. The incidence of transcription does not rob the poetry of its traditional dirge sentiments. The dirge is better realised in performance with audience interactions. But its expression in the written mode has gone a long way to preserve it for posterity. As Theo Vincent notes:

> ... the (written) word is certainly one of the most enduring ways of preserving ideas and memories. For after all the fever and heat of festivities, after the echoes of the dying footfalls of departing celebrants, the mementoes we come to cherish are those that transcend time.[10]

'Odogwu Kabral'

R. M. Ekechukwu's *'Odogwu Kabral, n'odu Mma'* achieves cognate effect with a panoply of proverbs and idioms spawning the lush richness of traditional environment. The poem begins with the proclamation, or announcement, as of the town crier and his gong:

Oji daa n'ala

---

[10] Theo Vincent ed., *Black and African Writing*, Lagos, Emacoprint Ltd, 1981, Introduction

Umu ntakiri alia ya elu
Osisi wughari chaa akwukwo
Ma ifuru wusachaa ala
Emechakwaa ya akpoo!

Ufufe bia ya akwatuo ya
Mkpu na akika ga enwe ya
Ndu bu osisi
Ihe bu ndu bu onwu
Onye nwuo taa o gaghi anwukwa echi[11]

When the great Iroko has fallen
Then little children can climb it
The tree can bloom with leaves
Or flowers, spread its branches
In the end, dry it must become

When the wind blows it shall fall
Anthills shall overtake it
Life is a tree
What life means is death (yet)
Whoever dies today shall never
die tomorrow
(Translation by the author)

Two stanzas introduce death as a phenomenon with striking paradox of life and death philosophically envisioned as two faces of the same coin. The image of life as a tree ('ndu bu osisi'), full of flowers and leafy branches that must

---

[11] R.M Ekechukwu, 'Odogwu Kabral n'odu mma' appeared in *Akpa Uche* an anthology of Igbo poems, Ibadan, Oxford Universty Press, 1975

nevertheless wither, serves to illustrate the impermanence of human conditions, and grimly foreshadows death. However, it is in the third stanza that the deceased hero is identified.

> *Kabral anwola O bu ezi okwu*
> *Ihi ala nna ya kwafuru ya*
> *Ala Afririka ahusiela anya*
> *Obiarabia ka onye nwe ala*
> *Emesiela anyi ike*

> Kabral is dead it is true
> Exiled from the face of his fatherland
> The land of Africa has suffered
> A guest more powerful than his host
> Has done evil to us.

His death is rightly interpreted by the poet as a loss to all of Africa. An Igbo proverb says that death is the guest who torments his host. Significantly, colonialism, against which Kabral relentlessly fought in his life time, is alluded to as a form of death, especially in the last stanza which bids farewell to the departed hero.

> *Amilka Kabral, n'odu mma-o...!*
> *Ebela akwa n'ala mmuo*
> *I di ndu ma taa*
> *Obiara na nke anyi si ya biagbuo anyi*
> *Ya lawa nkpukpu tokwee ya n'azu*

> Amilca Cabral, fare well
> Do not cry in the land of the dead

> For you live in the here-and-now
> The visitor who seeks to discomfiture us
> Shall carry a hunch back on his way home.

'*Odogwu Kabral, n'odu mma*' thereby achieves two effects as a dirge and political statement against colonial adventurism very much in character with its implacably vocal exponent Amilcar Cabral.

As an African dirge, it achieves its impact with proverb-studded idioms and imagery. For example, the poet speaks of Cabral's killers:

> *Agwo loro ibe ya*
> *Ahu anaghi adi ya mma*
> *Olee kwanu ebe onye gburu gi no ugbua?*
> *Gwa anyi ndi Portugal*
> *Mmuo kabral achufouola ya*

> The snake that swallows its kind
> Never regains its normal self
> Now where has your killer fled
> Tell us Portugal
> The spirit of Cabral haunts him

Yet the death of the hero contrasts with the victory over Portuguese colonialists

> *Obi di anyi uto*
> *Na ihe bere pii, anwuola*
> *Ihe ahu ijii ndu gi chuo aja*

Ike kwe ga abu nke gi
N'oge na-eteghi aka

Our hearts are gladdened
That what whimpered has now died
That, for which you sacrificed your life,
Will be yours, maybe
In not too distant time.

The poet's feeling is a mixed one, alternating between despondency at the loss of a great son of Africa (in the first two stanzas) and elation at the triumph of the hero's battle while on earth (in the subsequent ones). Death is a spiritual paradox of life; secularly, death becomes the extension of colonial oppression. Spurred by this later viewpoint, the attitude of the mourner takes on a political defiance. The people have suffered ('Ala Afririka ahuseila anya'), but they have come out the wiser because now the fight against death becomes the struggle against the colonial oppressor. The 'communal host' has decided that no longer shall he suffer humiliation at the hands of his own visitor. Again, like Chimezie, he wraps up this conviction with the proverb of his people which appears a more definitive action on the part of the poet:

Obiara na nke anyi si ya biagbuo anyi
Ya lawa nkpunkpu tokwee ya n'azu.

> (The visitor who seeks to undo us
> Shall carry a hunch back on his way home.)

The poem '*Odogwu Kabral*' can be read as a monologue in which the mourner is in a deep intra-personal communication. It therefore compares in passionate depth and emotional intensity of '*Onuma*' (Sorrows), and in its poetic evocation and mystical communion with Pol Ndu's 'Song for Seer.'

Both poems begin with silent rumination, a chewing over, as of the cud, of the deep philosophic meaning of dying and departure into the worlds unseen. It is a pattern that extends to a calling forth of the dead man's spirit-life, a mystical communication, and finally, the realisation that comes with the mourner's enlightenment on the significance of the death of the loved one for him, the mourner, and for his people or society in general. This comparison will emerge clearer with further study of African rhythms in 'Song for Seer.'

Chapter 4

African Rhythms in English

*A synthesis of forms *'Song for Seer' *'Lament in a Storm' *'The Story of a Ceylonese Girl' * 'Lament for the Dauntless Three'*

A synthesis of forms

Eldred Jones argues that the successful African poem must be the work of a poet with a sensibility well grounded in African traditions and who also has available to him techniques of development derived both from African and other traditions[1] Similarly, other African scholars have opted for the gradual evolution of African aesthetics which may incorporate some formal basic western literary forms such as characterisation, narrative technique, plot and style as in prose; or versification, rhyme and rhythm as in poetry, with traditional legacies of African oral literature.

What is proposed therefore is a synthesis of form and value –like what Chinua Achebe did to the modern African novel. Having 'domesticated' the English Language, the product is a new kind of English, at home with its native

---

[1] Eldred Jones, *African Literature Today Vol 10*, London, Heinemann Educational Books, 1979, p. 41

environment, but made to 'carry the weight' of the tradition, culture and values of the African world.[2]

Domestication as part of modern literary aesthetics offers a pragmatic approach to comparative appreciation of the literatures of Africa. First, it avoids the pitfalls of most prescriptive criticisms and secondly, it averts the error of polarisation of African literature between the extremes of Afro- and Euro-centricism.[3] Its method is thus more comparative than judicial or pontifical, more analytical than prescriptive. It is an approach by which the critic of African literature seeks to discover wider possibilities of influence, stylistic intertextuality, divergence, or points of distinction.

In the African dirge, what we try to do therefore is to appreciate individual poems within the totality of the dirge tradition in Africa. The poetic tradition in Africa is not seen in purely isolated context because domestication presupposes the validity of cross-cultural influences arising from borrowing or imitations and integration of two or more

---

[2] *See* Chinua Achebe 'The African Writer and the English Language' *Morning Yet on Creation Day*, London, Heinemann Educational Books Ltd, 1975, pp49-62.

[3] *See* Diana Brydon 'New Approaches to the New Literatures in English: Are we in Danger of Incorporating Disparity?' in Hena Maes-Jelinek et al ed., *A Shaping of Connections: Commonwealth Literature Studies - Then and Now*, Australia, Dangaroo Press, 1989, pp 89-99. *Also see* D.I Nwoga 'Modern African Poetry: The Domestication of a Tradition', in Eldred Jones ed., *African Literature Today, Vol 10*, London, Heinemann Educational Books, 1979, pp 32-56

cultural patterns into an overall (poetic) expression. The extent of success can then be evaluated by the extent which the vehicle of communication (English, French, Arabic or Portuguese languages) is acculturated into a wholistic African sensibility that includes its values, history and experiences, both individual and collective; a language, as Achebe puts it, that can be made

> to carry the weight of (the)... African experience ...still in full communion with its ancestral home but altered to suit its new African surroundings.[4]

For the African dirge in English we have inherited a poetic structure of stanzas and rhyme schemes. Indeed, the argument for an African aesthetics polarised along a 'traditional' or 'modern' dichotomy, or solely by the medium of expression, grows superfluous by the day. Okigbo himself did set this stage with 'Path of Thunder' when he said,

> we are trying to cast about for words. whether the words are in Igbo or English or in French is in fact immaterial ... we are looking for words to give verbal concreteness, to give verbal life to

---

[4] Chinua Achebe, *Morning Yet on Creation day*, p. 61

auditory and visual images.⁵

The creative product of this search ('casting about') can be felt in the haunting drone of the 'Elegy for Alto,'

> And the horn may now paw the air howling goodbye
> ...
> The Eagles are suddenly there
> new stars of iron dawn
> so let the horn paw the air howling goodbye.⁶

Pol Ndu refers to this development in African poetry as 'necessary.'

> The necessary development is that the
> African artist generates patent imagery
> and symbolism that capture his roots
> and sensibility in a distinctive style.⁷

He terms his own *Songs for Seers* as embodying a challenge to African roots and heritage. The poems become

> the ramifications of eschatological

---

⁵ D. I. Nwoga ed., *Perspectives on Okigbo*, Washington DC, Three Continents Press, 1984, p. 34

⁶ Christopher Okigbo, *Labyrinths*, U.S.A, Africana Publishing Corporation, 1971, p. 72

⁷ Pol Ndu, *Songs for Seers*, New York, NOK Publishers, 1974, Preface

> challenge to the African *Ofo*, the inevitable confrontation between the trappings of competing psycho-spiritual orders and a prophecy for a new circle from the historical realities...[8]

And he avers that it is naive to disdain influences in any form of artistic endeavour.

Agreeably, these influences run deep in the heritage and culture of modern African literature, expressed through careful observation and mastery of the forms of expression be they English or any other language.

'*Song for Seer*'

Pol Ndu's poem 'Song for Seer,' despite its fusions with elements of traditional rhetoricism, imagery and panegyric allusions, can be called the reflections of a mourner in English tradition. Its communication is both interpersonal (poet to Okigbo) in one, and intrapersonal (poet to himself) in the other —an indulgence the communal artist can hardly afford. He wants to be heard; he yells quite loudly.

---

[8] Pol Ndu, 1974, Preface

The poem 'Song for Seer,' a dirge on late Christopher Okigbo, begins with the parallel historical sense in the poet's reference to the deceased's own poem: 'Come Thunder.'

'The smell of blood that floats in the lavender mist' later becomes a prophetic anticipation. Okigbo ranks in the consciousness of the poet among the immortal beings who come once in an age to interact with the race of man.

> Minutes trickle thinly through, age:
> Where mortals with immortals share the stage.[9]

The device of rhetoricism may serve the purpose of the tragic sense, but here again the audience differs, the first is the deceased poet-hero;

> Who else could be the dying immortal
> but you
> Seated at heaven's gate!

The other is the poet as well as the deceased hero in a moment of overwhelming realisation.

> But why all the haste to the climax
> Knowing that star on ascent can never be split
> ...
> why all the lament...
> ...

---

[9] Pol Ndu, 1974, pp 16-17

knowing its deadness without your voice.

While 'Song' does not address a participatory and sympathetic audience, the poetic attitude to death is of deep personal significance in the monologue. The agony of loss is acute, yet subdued as it interacts, trance-like in haunting rhythms and subdued emotions, with the departed immortal soul of Okigbo.

> Who else,
> But you...
> You who heard and gave tongue
> The growls of thunder
> Listened and brought home the
> Songs of the water woman...
> You
> Who sat and sang
> Into the coldness of sacrificial nights.

The mystic sense is enhanced in the fourth stanza by the incantatory resonance achieved by combination of the long vowel sound /u:/ and the nasal /m/.

> Awaiting the millenni<u>um</u>
> After the ultimat<u>um</u>
> Of the day of <u>doom</u>

with the invocative appeal for the return of the immortal,

> Come back to this void
> Seed of seeing and knowing.

Okigbo is both seer and the razor-tongued weaver bird, and like most seers and visionaries, was heard (for his poetry), but not quite understood, the 'shackled citadel polished with tongs.' The poet experiments with sound effects and tonal rhythms in the same manner of his traditional counterparts.

> You f<u>ou</u>ght th<u>u</u>nder and
> F<u>ou</u>ght f<u>ame</u>
> L<u>o</u>st your fr<u>ame</u> and g<u>a</u>ve
> A n<u>ame</u> to fly
> Hi<u>gh</u>, hi<u>gh</u>er
> And hi<u>gh</u>est whence you
>
> <u>H</u>ired your blame

The simulation of mystical sublimity with the poetic decoration of language and subsequent 'transfiguration' of meaning with alliterations, assonance, repetitions and superlatives, sustains the supernaturalistic existence along with motifs of fire and other elements ('thunder,' 'flame' star,' 'flicker,') and flight ('ascent,' 'fly,' 'high,' 'higher' and 'highest,' 'haste').

Despite the ascent or departure of Okigbo beyond the void, the poet sustains his invocation for the return of his soul.

> Come among mortals
> Immortal man
> Move around your flicker
> ...
> however bitter.

We are bound in a consolation that the deceased dwells among immortals not so much by the incident of his death, as by the gift of sublime sensitivity through which his works have flickered to mortal men. Thus, within this overall structure of existence is an invisible bar of demarcation between the immortal vision of 'heaven's gate,' 'water woman' and the corporeal reality of 'bleak void,' faithless titans,' 'forked roads' and 'coldness of sacrificial nights.'

Since it takes the séance to communicate to the soul of the departed, the poet is therefore cut in the mode of a visionary. His song is poet-to-poet, the environment reaching from the familiar 'jam-dum dance' and 'such brevity at moon play,' through 'the void' to the realm of the immortality.

Even as an Anglophone writing, 'Song for Seer' will not belong to the English tradition of poetry as, needless to say, its heritage is rooted in its African world. In exercising the craft of transmuting private feelings and sensitivity to as public an issue as a dirge song to a celebrity, the poet as seer, employs the art of poetic invocation to some degree of success.

> Come back to this void
> Seed of seeing and knowing
> Razor-tongued weaverbird.

Ndu's song contributes to enrich African poetry. We may note literary rhyming and alliterations:

> *minutes trickle thinly through*   (/t/)
> *where mortals and immortals* (/o:/)
> *share the stage*
> ...
> *seed of seeing*   (/i:/)

We may also note the heavy rhythm and assonance inaugurated to achieve a magical incantation that momentarily conjures Igbo *ofo* chant,

> Pinned at forked roads
> awaiting the millennium
> after the ultimatum
> of the day of doom

With this panoply of sound and rhyme the progressive movement or ascent is almost climactic:

> Where you fought thunder
> ...
> fought flame lost your frame
> and gave a name
> ...
> to fly high higher and highest...

The poem enriches awareness of a deeply rooted Igbo heritage with language of English as vehicle for its creative expression. Central to its progress too is the prevailing reference to Okigbo as a source of literary influence.

> Seated at the limits of Heaven's gate
> ...who heard and gave tongue
> to the growls of thunder...
> and brought home
> the songs of the water-woman
> ... the manhood of the ram before Idoto
> ... he-goat-on-heat

Pol Ndu's poetry can thus be described as a testament to an enduring poetic tradition in Africa which meets the challenge of expressing contemporary themes and projecting personal feelings in a voice attuned both to its own culture and the heritage of western aesthetics.

'Lament in a Storm'

The writer of the Bible's 'Lamentation' leaves us with some of the finest poetry to come from Judaic tradition. This is an acknowledgement of the universality of artistic impulses triggered by actual disaster, or the sense of it.

> My eyes are spent with weeping
> my soul is in tumult
> my heart is poured out in grief
>
> ...
>
> because infants and babies faint
> in the streets of the city[10]

For Jeremiah, the catastrophe was in the fall of Jerusalem to the Chaldean army who vandalised the city and took the Jewish monarch and his nationals hostage. Jeremiah becomes the weeping prophet, our modern African equivalent of the dirge singer, lamenting the psychic devastation and physical destruction of his beloved nation:

> How lonely sits the city
> that was full of people
> How like a widow has she become
> she that was great among nations
> She that was a princess among the cities
> has become a vassal

---

[10] Lamentations, 2:11 *The Bible*, Revised Standard Version.

The Jeremiad of T. C. Nwosu cannot but be obvious. The patriotic sentiment and love of motherland is evident in both writings. Biafra, which Chris Okigbo laid down his life for, personified to Nwosu, and most Igbo, what Jerusalem meant to the Jews. The title of lament in Nwosu's is more than a fleeting confluence with the lamentation of Jeremiah in the Bible. Nwosu's arcane language, full of syntactic parallelisms, is certainly biblical.

Yet, even as far such comparisons go 'Lament in a Storm' can be seen in the context of an African dirge song which rhythm is essentially an African 'beat' and which medium is as Nwoga says of modern African poetry:

> though its language is English, the elements of its background are the total environment of today's Africa; its tradition a convoluting mixture of the basic African origins and the inspiring catalyst of borrowed models.[11]

Nwosu's voice casts the familiar image of the African obituary announcer with his gong. The poet's emotional involvement in the death of Okigbo can be seen in the friendship and comradeship both had shared in their private and professional calling as poets.

---

[11] Eldred Jones ed., *African Literature Today Vol. 10,* London, Heinemann Educational Books Ltd, 1979, p. 53

There are eight parts in this long lamentation; each in a stanza that flows through the subsequent ones. There are no choruses as in Chimezie's 'Ebelebe.' The first part stanza introduces the elements, flora and fauna of weeping nights, forests with broken wings, crying birds, groaning earth and sobbing wind. The poet laments amidst this confusion:

> Songs have sold their meanings
> they now wear the willow only wailing dirges
> remain
> to mock the memory
> to make the beat of the muffled drum
> rise to melt the senses.[12]

Dirge songs and dances are mourning instruments in this African world. The lamentations that fill the land are sharp painful reminders of the death of Okigbo. It is the medium of poetic (drum) communication. In part II, the mourner, having set the mood, goes on to recount history: the events of the war that took the life of his friend.

> It was during the days of the sword
> when we were under the vast
> Net that mad ambition
> had flung over us...

---

[12] Chinua Achebe and Dubem Okafor ed., *Don't Let Him Die*, Enugu, Fourth Dimension Publishers, 1978, pp.24 - 27

Okigbo is made to represent, by extension, all that his people of Biafra had stood for: 'a blade of steel' underestimated as 'mere butterfly;' an oasis marooned by its own neighbours in a desert of dust and sand. This recapitulation of the past is aptly presented in English structural pattern of Subject/ Predicator/ Complement (SPA/A) followed repetitively with Adjunct parallels.

It/was/ during the days of the sword/
S P

when we were under the vast
net that made ambition
/has flung over us/
      A

when some thought you were
/a mere butterfly.../
      A

When an oasis was marooned
/In a desert of dust and sand.../
      A

When you stretched out
/In a trench to wear out a night.../
      A

Repetition of 'when' with the recurrence of the Adjunct (A) situates the event correctly in the past, and yet gives immediacy and clarity to such recollection. It is made to link sonorously, in unbroken sequence, to the third stanza of part III.

Here, the new structure is rhetorical questioning: 'Who could have...' is repeated twice

/who/ /could have thought/
   S   P

that a bird, your friend
/nested close to your bed/
        C

/who/ /could have believed/
   S   P

/that your own would fall upon you/
        C

And is concluded by the recurring Adjunct (A) 'with' also (two times).

/with the cold naked blade/
   A

/with rifles and mortars/
   A

In part IV, the poet continues mourning for the man lost in the war. Only his song remains now to assuage the bitterness of the whole injustice of war. This is introduced by the word 'lest' which is repeated twice:

> Lest our grief should stir
> The gloom about us
> ... ...
> Lest our land should tremble
> With her furious sighing...

This poet's technique of structural parallelism constantly re-emphasises the tragic feeling meant to be conveyed in the overall poem for it simulates the act of weeping with each recurrence.

In part V, the historical sense of Part II is again evoked with 'once' (occurring twice). But this time, it is a historical flight of fancy and product of the dirge imagination. The African poetic universe traverses the physical into an incorporeal universe. But for the poet, it is a poetic universe cultured with western royalty: of 'lavender-scented streets,' 'perfumed waters,' 'bosomed garlands' --a hallucinatory world in which the deceased has bathed luxuriantly 'surrounded by the homage of three thousand devoted servants....' It is the universe of previous Okigbo poetry, which his poet-colleague calls:

> Prodigal, prodigal echoes of the life of a he-
> man...

and which won for 'the prodigal'

> 'white petals of fame,' because he sang
> ... songs
> that blushed many a cheek
> and made them seek to lay laurels
> At (his) solemn feet.

The poet by acting as a critic of his colleague employs one of the most effective methods of traditional dirge performance: the art of dramatic censure. At a funeral ceremony, a mourner suddenly changes to total irritation. What follows is a stream of abuses for the dead man's carelessness in matters of finance. And what was the reaction of sympathisers? Pity. As some of them put it, 'it really touched the young man.'

T. C. Nwosu, in narrating the loss of his friend

Okigbo, also finds himself at this point of hysteria and he employs poetic dialogue with the departed hero.

> You were a cathedral column
> that could have soared up erect
> without end, before your return
> home, your own home, for your final
> sleep!

The dialogue on Okigbo's poetic style of 'passive resistance in stylish silence,' poetically tagged 'Satyagraha' continues in Parts VI and VII; the mourner wails in the rhetorical mode.

> Was it ripe for poling your canoe
> for reaching the shore
> where dark turtles come to feed,
> Where the boat man frightens, is
> frightened
> by untimely demise?...

The effect of lexical parallelisms employed in this rhetoric is made to permeate the entire structure of this dirge. In the concluding part, the rhetoricism ends with the effect of a whimper: 'what...' (repeated twice).

> What flood can wash
> over these thoughts?

> What can thaw the gasps
> of this breath, the stormy throb
> of this heart ?

Double and triple repetitions of key phrases in the structure of the language vehicle are significant of overwhelming emotions and continue to the last lines:

> Nothing, nothing.

The general success of the poem lies in its sustenance of the emotive sensitivity, the feeling of loss, pain and injustice. The overall sadness and deep cogitation of the singular tragic plight go beyond linguistic barriers to appeal to the emotion of the listener and elicit the mournful sorrowing that is occasioned by death.

If we scan the range of available imagery, we will distinguish two parallels of Western and African motifs. The images of 'willow,' 'lavender,' 'fountain,' 'bosomed garlands,' 'threaded yellow and orange flowers,' 'white petals,' 'cheeks blushed,' 'laurels laid on feet,' 'cathedral column,' and 'Satyagraha' reflect the western poetic sensibility associated with the early Okigbo poetry.

However, the prevalent images of 'forest's broken wings,' 'birds cried,' 'earth groaned,' 'sobbed with the wind,' 'muffled drum,' 'canoe poling,' 'reaching the shore,' 'dark turtles' and 'frightened boat man' (associations of death in traditional African mythology) all serve to establish the roots of the lamentation in an essentially African world. Furthermore, the realisation (in part) of the poem through the African mode of dirge rendition also entrenches the poem within the African milieu.

The poet in furthering these objectives has expressed a subtle preference for his own natural cultural landscape in his attribution of the early Okigbo as 'prodigal echoes.' His similes and metaphors are drawn from the celebrated home of 'forests, broken wings, crying birds...' 'The men at war were huddled together

>'like sheep in a pen,'

the betrayer of Okigbo, and indeed Biafra is cast in the metaphor of

>a bird (that) nested close to your bed

the gloom of grief and defeat is

>like a thick black fog/blown about in the night

The poet communicates the natural rhythms of African mourning and lament.

'The Story of a Ceylonese Girl'

'The Story of a Ceylonese Girl' by Ossie Enekwe explores the traditional dirge chorus, a mode of poet-audience interaction which is realised here by the use of repetitions. As in Chimezie's 'Okigbo Ebelebe Egbuole,' the chorus in 'Ceylonese Girl' may be sung by an audience.

In the dirge poem, Mathi Kulersegaram, a Ceylonese undergraduate of the University of Nigeria, Nsukka dies fighting for Biafra during the war. The dirge casts her death as something fated by destiny. Kulersegaram is certainly one of precious humanity destroyed in the genocide that characterised war and other savageries of mankind.

> She heard the music of eternity
> ... ...
> she rode on the wings of the wind crushed and drowned in a restless sea[13]

Some of Enekwe's dirge poems 'The Story of a Ceylonese Girl,' 'To a Friend made and lost in the War,' 'Husbandman' are marked by detailed narrative sequence where the circumstantial details about the hero/heroine are amply highlighted in a manner of poetic exploration. Mathi Kulersegaram's blood is

---

[13] Ossie Enekwe, *Broken Pots*, New York, Greenfield Review Press, 1977, p.2

> Polluted by battle powder
> skull and bones of a Biafra lover
> left to smoulder and crack in the flames
> of a city whose path she loved to walk.

We are told that her death must be an act of the gods because although she 'should have gone to her mother,' like most foreigners did at the outbreak of the war, she rejected that option. Her love for Biafra and the ideals it stood for however became a

> ... casing
> to take her well to the clay
> beyond the reaches of the people she loved so much
> far away from the dust of her own dear land.

The poem also provides the circumstance for a philosophical reflection on the tragic phenomenon. As in Igbo traditional verse (Abigbo), death is dressed in the image of darkness:

> ... the wind of eternity
> dark traces dancing in the gloom

Hence each of the four stanza verse, including the

short chorus of two lines, is a development of the tragic image in the persona of the Ceylonese girl.

> ... sad music of a wasted life
> mirrored on the furrows of a pretty face

Enekwe calls his poem a song for the guitar, thereby confirming that the poem is meant to achieve its fullest realisation with musical accompaniment. On this, Edith Ihekweazu rightly remarks that in Enekwe's poems, 'we find strong elements of performance and acting. Many pieces,' she avers 'are explicitly called songs and more than once we find reference to poetry as singing.[14] In performance, we can visualise the poet-artiste leading the chant with his guitar or some other apt musical instrument while the chorus follows in the background with the refrain:

> This is the story of a Ceylonese girl
> This is the story of Kulersegaram

Such dramatic interpolation may occur at (I) the end of the four-stanza lead chant, or (ii) the end of each stanza of the song. In either case, what is important is that we have an active audience in participation and, in this instance, there may be little or no distinction between listeners and chorus.

---

[14] Ossie Enekwe, 1977, Foreword

Furthermore, the leader with the guitar is much like the singer in African-American blues:

> Blood of Mathi Kulersegaram
> polluted by battle powder
> skull and bones of a Biafra lover
> left to smoulder and crack in the flames
> of a city whose paths she loved to walk faraway
> from the people she loved so much

The poetry is descriptive and paints a scenario of war and bloodshed.

> Blood of Mathi Kulersegaram
> ....
> skull of a Biafra lover

continuing into the second stanza in alternating syntactic parallels:

> she heard the music of eternity
> way down the depth of her soul
> she rode on the wings of the wind
> like a flower rushed in a storm
> in a land growing grassless from a scorching sun

In stanza three;

> Mathi should have gone to her mother
> not try to stop a falling rock
> Mathi's love was the casing to take her well to the clay

And stanza four;

> Mathi will never come again
> ...
> she is gone with the wind of eternity
> dark traces dancing in the gloom ...

The poem's appeal to our emotions does not necessarily lie in the tragedy of war, as the general thematic pre-occupation. The 'grassless land' in the 'scorching air/crushed and drowned in a restless sea; 'the flames of a city' and the 'falling rock' become signposts to ultimate national as well as personal tragic destiny:

> Like a flower rushed in a storm
> ... ...
> crushed and drowned in a restless sea.

By this tragic fate, the poem spilts in two parts each containing two stanzas. Each beginning line of the first two stanzas, in part, starts on the descriptive note

> Blood of Mathi Kulersegaram
> ...
> She heard the music of eternity
> ...

while the lines of the last two stanzas in Part 11 begin with a sort of declamation

> Mathi should have gone back to her mother
> ...
> Mathi will never come back again
> ...

In the second part, the poet tells us the enduring qualities of the ill-fated stranger: Stanza III

> Mathi's love was the casing
> to take her well to the clay
> beyond the reaches of the people she loved so much
> far away from the dust of her own dear land.

In stanza IV, the departure precipitated by that tragic choice in stanza III is complete:

> She is gone with the wind of eternity
> dark traces dancing in the gloom
> to the sad music of a wasted life
> mirrored on the furrows of a pretty face.

The chorus would now conclude the movement with the final whimper. A dramatic quality which has been noted of Ossie Enekwe's poems could be heightened by the dying voices and fading light as the chorus ends the song with

> This is the story of a Ceylonese girl
> This is the story of Kulersegaram

'Ceylonese Girl' is no doubt a poem of wide literary dimensions and the influences go beyond the immediate Nigerian environment and even the African world. In his composition, he has taken some of the nuances of the blues, the feeling of sadness and longing, the melancholy that comes with departure, separation and consequently nostalgia and longing are heavily resonant. The effect is a powerful dirge song.

> like a flower crushed in a storm
> in a land growing grassless from scorching air
> crushed and drowned in a restless sea
>
> ...gone with the wind of eternity
> dark traces dancing in the gloom
> to the sad music of a wasted life
> mirrored on the furrows of a pretty face

The poetic evocation of one of the many casualties of that African tragedy affords us an elaborate dramatic performance combined with singing. The result of this experimentation is the new poetry that constantly enriches the widening arena of African influences. This is another form of domestication of a tradition. But in this case it is rather the incorporation of traditions and the assimilation of literary forms ranging from a variety of cultural landscapes.

'Lament for the Dauntless Three'

The poet of 'Lament for a dauntless three' occupies a significant position among experimenters of the new tradition both for the message and content of his poetry and his creative manipulation of oral traditions beyond the latter-Okigbo experiment. *Energy Crisis*,[15] his first volume of poetry marks Chinweizu's distinguishing temperament by his interest in people, their different mannerisms, peculiar characteristics and sensibilities as may be reflected in their responses to the society. His poems reflect the artiste's individual exposure and interpretation of various segments of society.

Invocations and Admonitions, his second volume of poems, marks his fervent Afrocentricism. The poet

---

[15] Chinweizu, *Energy Crisis and other Poems* Lagos: Nok Publishers, 1978

combines oral techniques of expression with the various traditional forms which serve to enrich African art. At this stage Chinweizu had unabashedly become the proponent for auditory poetry which 'places a high value on lucidity, normal syntax and precise and apt imagery,'[16]

In 'Lament for a dauntless Three,' the artiste's voice takes after the panegyric lamentation. This form of dirge which Ogunba identifies as being mainly in 'praise of heroes who have finally been defeated by the almighty spirit called death'[17] is seen as a form of inheritance by R. N. Egudu who posits that,

> Our modern poets have inherited from the Igbo traditional lamentations where the poet is full of praises for the dead man[18].

'Lament for a dauntless three' is doubtlessly full of praises for three heroes of Nigerian national history: Christopher Okigbo, Chukwuma Nzeogwu, and Murtala Mohammed. The heroes are typically cast in mythic

---

[16] Chinweizu et al *Toward the Decolonisation of African Literature*, Enugu, Fourth Dimension, 1980 p. 247

[17] Oyin Ogunba 'Traditional African Poetry' in a *Journal of the Nigeria English Studies Association*, Vol. 8, No. 2, December 1976, p. 45

[18] R. N. Egudu, 'The Art of Igbo Written Poetry,' a paper presented at the seminar on Igbo Art and Music, University of Nigeria, Nsukka, August 21-25, 1976, p15

dimensions, full of presumed goodness. They are usually those who had elevated the material well being of their people, helping the poor or making peace and justice reign. Their death is made to acquire a high tragic dimension that is intended to further exacerbate rather than console or palliate the emotions.

Chinweizu recreates this successfully, having painted a country in a riotous situation where

> thuggery raped the thighs of trustful
> nights/power turning petty flogged
> our laughter/peace flees...(and) the
> ship of state (rocks) in a flood...

The landscape becomes consequently ripe for 'a weaver bird (that) flew among us, a panther (that) sprang among us/ a lion (that) roared among us...'

Okigbo is decked in local fauna: a strong and courageous panther who leapt to 'scatter the granary thieves' and Murtala is the 'strong arm' that rose to clear the 'debris' of political misrule. These qualities set the stage for the tragedy of their deaths. When Okigbo is slain in the battlefield and left to 'wander in the forests of final nights,' and Nzeogwu is 'betrayed, trapped and gored,' and Murtala is later cut down by 'bullets sent to fetch his head,' a situation of utter despair and hopelessness is most powerfully projected:

> What voice shall comfort us…
> …
> what arm shall strike for us
> …
> what hand shall cleanse this rot…

The poet proceeds to recreate the search motif in Igbo funeral occasion. The deceased is not really dead until a thorough search has been conducted around the familiar places the deceased usually frequented during his lifetime. Now we join the mourning party for Nzeogwu who have

> …sifted the smoke of battle
> …
> Searched the trampled bushes
> Searched war camps in heaven

Similarly, the Murtala team:

> …have sifted the gun smoke
> Beaten the bush of the savannah
> Followed to the desert edge…

And the mourning procession for Okigbo,

> ... searched the fennel branches
> Searched song halls in heaven

The search is communal, denoted by 'we,' thus establishing the importance of the heroes to their community. It is mythically a futile one too. None of the heroes can be found in those places, thus establishing the tragic fact of their demise. A critic has suggested that Chinweizu's heroes are not good enough for heaven[19] by the futility of this 'search,' but this assumption is clearly incorrect.

In the lament, the tragic news 'chilled the ears' and even 'multitudes on the Niger bank ... raised a great lament.' This hyperbolic element raises the theme to tragic heights involving not only mourner but all in the community who are so affected. This is because the African funeral evokes,

> responses and interjections and small outbursts from other celebrants who serve as the chorus to the whole ritual.[20]

'Lament for the dauntless three' is not only an example of African dirge poetry celebrating the fallen heroes

---

[19] Stanley Amah, 'Chinweizu: Proclivity to the Profane,' in *The Journal of the Association of Nigerian Authors*, 1986, p. 13

[20] Kofi Awoonor, 1975, p. 102

but a part of an ongoing experimentation in the fusion of the traditional and modern.

It is by the examples of these selected poems that one may seek to establish a framework of the African dirge in its total content while taking cognition of all its possible forms of expression and style.

Chapter 5

Modern Dirge Voices

*The laments of younger poets * A Sense of betrayal in Letter to Lynda * Bitterness in Songs of a Market Place * The Acerbity of An African Eclipse * After-Loss in Naked Testimonies * Areas of artistic convergence*

The Laments of younger poets

Africa's history of poverty and political instability has triggered several laments by her poets through her 'series of jagged and traumatic sufferings.'[1] Since the human drain and agonies of the slave traffic and the colonial /post-colonial betrayal of the true aspirations of her people, the continent has been blighted with reversals of social, political and economic fortunes. Her sufferings are recorded everywhere but with especial poignance and clarity in her poetry all through the early and contemporary periods of her chequered life.

These brands of dirge poetry are expressed in the

---

[1] Basil Davidson, *The Black Man's Burden: Africa and the Curse of the Nation State*, Ibadan: Spectrum Books, 2000. p. 21

local voice of their environment despite the modernity of their styles. Our interest in these poems is their exploration of the idea of generational loss in their threnodies which styles of rendition draw from every sphere of human endeavour. It could be the loss sustained from betrayal of trust, disappointment in relationships, denial and deprivation of rights and atrophy of dreams.

Although it may be argued that these feelings are not as acute and desperate as those occasioned by death, yet lamentation poetry explores similar sentiments as the dirge, resulting in the convergence of moods. Wherever a poet utilises the threnodic voice in his poetry, such poems differ in terms of the sentiments expressing despair, gloom, hopelessness, melancholy, despondency, discouragement, bitterness, desperation, and shock. These feelings are also expressed through a language of ire, anger, passion, fury, exasperation, trepidation, blighted hope, pessimism, cynicism, bitterness, sarcasm, satire, ridicule, derision, irony, grief, distress, misery, woe, and anguish.

Most good poetry achieve harmony and meaning where surface layers of poetic expression yield its underlying innuendoes and medium. This perfect blend of medium and message, where successful in the hands of the poet, becomes the measure of the beauty of his verse.

But equally important is the relevance of a poet's art

within a given time and age. T. S. Eliot has been quoted as saying:

> the great poet, in writing himself, writes his time. It is the poet's business to express the greatest emotional intensity of his 'time' based on whatever his time happened to think.[2]

By extension, many of the younger poets today have become lamenters of their continental miseries. They bewail the atrophy of the dream and aspirations envisioned by their few leaders of thought. To this group belong such poets as Chinweizu, Funso Aiyejina, Ezenwa Ohaeto, Ossie Enekwe, Niyi Osundare and, more recently, Peter Onwudinjo, Toyin Adewale, Chin Ce, Ismail B. Garba, Remi Raji, Osita Ezeliora and Agwu Ude all from Nigeria.

After the upheavals of the nineteen sixties which degenerated into civil war, Nigerian poets continue the interrogation of their experiences after the fact. Even for the later group of poets such as Toyin Adewale and Chin Ce who belong to the generation born into the strife and tagged the *ogu eri dike*[3] age grades, the interrogation of history is a stronger imperative.

---

[2] John Hayward ed. 1963, p 23

[3] P. K Davids, *Igbo Names and Age Grading*, Handel Books, Enugu: 2000 p. 34

Generally, these poets lament the betrayal of the people's genuine aspirations for a better life, poverty, unemployment and the dilapidated state of the nation's economy. Their anger over the vicious cycle of brutality that diminishes the continent is unmistakable. It is this form of threnody ushered by these young men that has come to be known as the new generation poetry:

> Where are you oh Olokun
> They rape you and raid your children
> They march on your fertile brows
> And rig rods of crude pain in your veins[4]

These are the brand of poets whose impatience with nationalist slogans that fly in the face of glaring contradictions is hardly disguised. For them, political sloganeering is meaningless with strings of betrayal from their own body of leaders. The racial divide no longer holds water in a nation where the individual has, perhaps, never been more recently traumatised by any other generation or race than theirs.

This betrayal finds evidence in a history of civil war and post-war ethnic divisions and rivalries not to talk of other political legacies as inflation, crumbling educational institutions, rising corruption and sheer political bufoonery.

---

[3] Remi Raji, *Webs of Remembrance*, Kraft Books, Ibadan: 2000 p. 34

> Great ancestors of Ejimoke
> Mourn the silting and the trickle
> Of a house that thundered once
> Like youthful stream
> ...
> Today laughter is snuffed
> Out of the fireplace...[5]

These new African poets react to these times with disillusionment and sometimes utter contempt for the failed experiments with nation-statism in Africa such as Nigeria's. The hallmark of this brand of poetry as opposed to those of earlier generations includes their militancy of spirit often contrasted with the threnody of their voice. Both manners of poetic expression are informed by the higher visionary pursuits of these poets. The dearth of ethics in all spheres of the life of the nation is too overwhelming an issue to concatenate in 'mild' language, hence they 'scream out' these problems in a voice that is discernible to the masses whose woes they chronicle.

> Woe to you who plunder our peace
> And cast the jewels of our love

---

[5] Peter Onwudinjo, *Women of Biafra and other Poems*, DoubleDiamond, Port-Harcourt: 2000, p. 59

[6] Peter Onwudinjo, p. 86

To beasts and birds of prey
You will pay a dreadful price.[6]

The disillusionment and frustration brought about by these experiences inform the mood and tone of their poetry.

Betrayal: *Letter to Lynda*

Funso Aiyejina is one of the foremost new Nigerian poets. His collection of poems, *Letter to Lynda* appeared in 1984, blazing a trail in rhythms and discourse. Through such poems as 'Growing up', 'Before the dawn dawns,' and 'The year of hopeless-hope' the poet laments contemporary politics. The political themes of these poems are drawn from a desultory Nigerian nation state and the predatory instincts of their rulers. His poetry projects the mistrust, disillusionment, and disaster of the political experiments of the nation. The poet fiercely castigates those responsible for Nigeria's political and economic problems. Where death, in traditional dirge, is responsible for the demise of a loved one; the politicians are held responsible for the symbolic death of the nation state.

Till date this political anomaly persists through the continent and the dirge poets may crow themselves hoarse. Nigerian politicians still rig elections in blatant violation of constitutional ethics. To the poet, we are being herded towards mined futures because those whom we thought we voted into power derisively tell us to 'go and feed on (our) votes,' boasting shamelessly that 'they were victors long before the people voted.' For the masses, these conditions crystallise in a powerful sense of hopelessness. Just like somebody stung by death, the sensitivity of the poet stung by political and military despotism sees a bleak future ahead for the nation.

Both civilians and military rulers further heighten the feeling of despair in view of their rabid struggle for power so that the power baton merely vacillates between the vultures and their predatory kinds. Therefore, while 'pot-bellied speculators (with) ballot boxes (are on) the corridors of power (the) boot steps ... beat in wait /for (another) chance in our kingdom of chance.' None portends any good for the nation as 'our benevolent guardians personalise our fortunes into coded vaults ... (and) join ... in looting the (nation's) treasury dry.'

Having drained our coffers dry, they turn round to demand 'donations (from us) to refill them.' To divert attention from their crimes, they sow seeds of discord among the people. Now, 'our grown-up streets are paved with decimated oppositions.' And more recently these 'decimated oppositions' have taken the turn of sponsored religious killings.

The atrocities committed by Nigerian rulers against the populace would rather overwhelm even the crudest mediaeval sensitivity. But the bard is not astounded by his sorrow. The poet, motivated by an urgent need for reform, urges sagacity. He cautions us to 'fear the living (and) not the dead' as the fate of the 'living' at present is more shrouded in mystery than that of the 'dead.'

The need for this caution arises from the poet's charge that the military who came to 'rescue' us from the greed of the civilians failed us over and over. Funso Aiyejina sees military interventions as 'a gift of tragedy.' Military intervention in Africa's leadership is an experiment in failure and therefore should not be repeated. The masses once mistook the military rulers for real saviours and have been 'too dumbstruck to find a melody.'

Bitterness: *Songs of a Market place.*

Niyi Osundare's 'Siren' and 'Rithmetic of Ruse' explore similar political themes with Aiyejina's. Adopting an attitude of bitterness 'Siren' bewails the arrogant parade of power by our leaders. The poet is shocked that in spite of the people's love of state, and hope in their leaders, these leaders betray their trust.

> kwashiorkored children
> waving tattered flags, land
> disembowelled by erosion
> ... yam tendrils yellowing
> on tubers smaller than a palm kernel,

Their 'Excellencies' (manage not to see) the seeds of tomorrow's famine (because) they are not (there) for the begging bickering of the faceless rural crowd. The mourner of our national tragedy is a satirist who sketches the depressing poverty of the Nigerian people. Nevertheless, the poet reiterates the fact that whether they (the rulers) choose to notice it or not, the contorted babies on their 'mothers' back/ are question marks for tomorrow's answer.'

Osundare's lamentation is an example of the revolutionary temper that has fast become a dominant attitude in current dirge poetry. Instigated by the abject poverty of good leadership in the society, the feeling of loss and frustration grows acute, although the hope for mitigation is expressed at the end.

Similarly, 'Rithemetic of ruse' shows how power-hungry civilians inflate census figures in order to gain political advantage over their rivals politicians go to the extent of adding their cattle to census figures. They engage in all sorts of deceit in order to grab power. Osundare's poetry creates a feeling of despondency in the reader. But undaunted by these evil acts, the poet warns that the perpetrators of such crimes will not go unpunished. He is confident that they would be consumed by their deceit, 'leaving us with our search/for the fragments of truth.'

We clearly understand that these hardships existing in the nation-states of Africa, mainly from political power struggle, rigging, squandering of treasury, exploitation of local resources and deliberate fomentation of suspicion among ethnic groups, justifiably inform the African poet's lament in a society where art is both functional and entertaining.

The Acerbity of *An African Eclipse*.

In Chin Ce's *Eclipse*, poetry is in the service of society, not of necessity, but for the relevance of its making. Here, poetry is not merely the 'spontaneous overflow of powerful feelings,' it is a calculated, creative response of talent to environment. In this light, the poetry of Chin Ce reveals shared experiences in addition to a singular destiny whether collective or personal.

An African Eclipse appears like a song but bristles directly with constant reassessment of the past, while the poetic conviction is acute till its point of detonation in 'The

Prodigal drums.' Yet the overall threnody of the verse qualifies it as a modern African dirge poetry.

The prologue comprises a single poem 'Farewell,' wherein the poet sets the tone for a new direction. 'A Farewell' takes a decision on this visionary direction.

> But I have taken now the day is bright
> (the shining light of
> Soul lights) the other route.[7]

We may assume that this is a parting of ways, from old to new. Yet it is the 'old ways' that Chin Ce confronts us with in this poetry. Like a traditional bard, the poet in 'African Eclipse' mourns the atrophy of Africa's future. It is the truncation of hopes for a great black African nation by the 'generation without a soul,' in other words, an accursed generation. The poet puts the responsibility on military and civilian collaborators in the politics of national ruination.

The tendency to load the enemy with all kinds of negative images has become a continuing tradition with most poetry of lamentation. Nigerian politicians are vultures, and their military turncoats are reptiles. In any case, the military are the precipitators of the eclipse. In 'Darkness,' the poet leaves us in no doubt of the vicious wheel of counter military interventions around which the nation was made to

---

[7]Chin Ce, *An African Eclipce*, Handel Books, Enugu: 2000, p. 3

revolve for several decades of its history. 'All borders closed' is only but 'blundering in the dark.' Metaphorically, this darkness is similar to the benumbed feeling of total loss and desolation experienced at the instance of death. In other words the country is dead politically.

> time only crawled
> ...
> and who began to curse?

By this rhetoricism the poet admonishes the Nigerian masses (whom he indicts as being passive) to ignore or refrain from giving support to the meddlesome interlopers: 'Let us stretch and yawn/like late risers of early morn.'

Yet the most acerbic lamentation of political corruption can be found in the four-part movement of the 'Eclipse.' 'The sun shall not wait...' begins the poet, in admonitory locution to a (typically Nigerian) president who barricades himself in office and is now alienated from his people. The image of time which does not wait but hurtles down the decline is ominous of impending doom:

> Time does not stall
> It hurtles
> Dangerously down the decline
> And every penny must be paid

> For every spill of blood
> And that smack on the cheek
> For the humiliation of one man
> And diminution of his dignity⁹

Past and present leaderships, as the poet bemoans, have been intrinsically self-serving. The president, in his 'drunken dream' of office accoutrements fondles his mistresses behind the primitive seclusion of his estate. In some cases, all he volunteers are mere speeches and unoriginal public declarations. To his retinue of sycophants, he offers bacchanal feasts and medals of service, which the poet-mourner scorns as 'dog medals around their necks.'

In contrast to this affluence are the wretched people: 'bearers/of the land's loads.' Of course such sights as 'bony heads of children,' and homeless street dwellers are safely shut from the view of Nigeria's number one public official who does not see very much from his seat of indulgence. Apart from empty slogans, Nigerian leadership further insults the people's intelligence with human rights violations, extortion and murder by corrupt police and uniformed security personnel.

> Cries of torture and murder
> Sweep the streets
> Where your mad dogs roam

---

⁸Chin Ce, *An African Eclipce*, p.19

The poet, in the manner of a visionary, warns of dire consequences. Time, is no respecter of persons. The style of rendition, presents time as the great leveller: that which equalises the imbalance among men, nations, and races. 'Every penny must be paid,' is the refrain that warns the abusers of public trust of the consequences to come. This may be in the form of civil disobedience

> the day your requiem is sung
> ...
> In your face picture patch
> Of what a crook has done this land

or, worse still, a social upheaval. But the effect of this turn-around would mean the civic act of public unmasking. 'Every spill of blood,' and humiliation of men, will, like the proverbial chicken, come home to roost as it did for the despot in 'The Epitaph.'

There are certainly other locales of the eclipse in both historical and imaginative landscapes of the poet. 'Sob' records some other stained spots of the continent, including two other poems on the South African experience. Like the Nigerian eclipse, the South African state led by majority blacks threatens to extinguish the spirit of African brotherhood by its xenophobic aggressiveness towards both black and white.

> Thunder in Transkei
> chars in Ciskei
> Burnt bleached terrain
> And remnants only...
>
> Broken minds and battered bodies
> Litter the trail
> After violence
> In Soweto[10]

This theme of the violence of apartheid proceeds to the second part. Yet black-against-black violence continues even after majority rule. This contradiction of purpose comes too soon after South African independence has been won on clouds of 'thunder' and 'bellows.'

Other renditions in *African Eclipse* include two poems to the novelist, Chinua Achebe. In 'Wind and Storm,' Yeatsan holocaust and twentieth century confusion come up again under the whirling wind.

> Wind and storm are whirling
> In a land dis-eased
> Many things fall apart [11]

If the poet agrees with Yeats, it however, lies not in the apocryphal vision of the latter, nor in socio-cultural confusion of the former's generation. Rather in 'Wind and

---

[10] Chin Ce, *An African Eclipce*, p.21
[11] Chin Ce *An African Eclipce*, p.29

Storm,' the confusion of twenty-first century Africa is due to the very machinations of her leaders against their own kind. Greed and avarice destroy a nation. Therefore, in the flight of an Achebean arrow, the poet encapsulates a staunch philosophic idea with artistic virtuosity: Man is the architect of his own downfall. 'They pierced their own hearts,' the poet deposes, 'one hundred million minions.'

The poignant point of this threnody is the varied critical assessment of the Nigerian society. In 'Prodigal Drums,' the poet exposes the average Nigerian through Fuff who represents the juvenile dereliction of moral values.

Fuff's boisterous, happy-go-lucky city life creates a tension of opposing forces of conformity and rebellion which snaps very soon, and predictably too. Fuff's rebellion (Nigeria's social existence) is uncoordinated, one-man squad, not founded on a strategic base yet just enough to make a victim of the hero. No resistance to such a corrupt society that Nigeria offers can be successful by just one man's indignation and physical protest. The society that breeds corrupt electricity officials, police officers, judges, etc., ensures that Fuff, one of its rebels, permanently remains behind bars until his mental derangement. The loneliness of Fuff comes across in pithy lines.

There was no one, not one

> to pay the bail
> and for nine hundred weeks
> far in the northern heat
> did the sun of the Sahara
> blank his mind in jail[12]

Fuff returns with obvious mental and fiscal disability cast in a grotesque sense of humour: 'robbed again: wad and sense.' Later in the lament, Fuff's misplaced aggression grows both comic and pithy. His aggression towards mother and father, including a faceless society, cannot but evoke bitter laughter.

> Where am I?
> the stone the builders rejected
> and by Bacchus with my machete
> shall I have your heads for dinner.

The uncomfortable non resolution of the conflict is deliberate, for the tension of the ruler and the governed cannot but ultimately snap in the darkness of betrayals and misdirected priorities.

But *African Eclipse* is not all a lament about 'stinging stench,' 'stalking hyenas,' 'barbarian and his boot,' and 'tired drummers.' The epilogue that hints at some future determination, is symbolic of an after-eclipse. The sun in the epilogue amplifies the concept even before the succeeding four poems enforce this hope of a renewal. More striking to

---

[12] Chin Ce *An African Eclipce*, p.39

the critical sensibility is how the mourner-poet presents this sense of renewal *aposterori*. In the loud denunciations of the preceding section, none could have thought such deep sense of optimism possible. But here is the real vintage of an African lamentation that lifts the veil of sullen grief to reveal a landscape of glorious fortune.

After-Loss: *Naked Testimonies*

According to Toyin Adewale, *Naked Testimonies* starts on a night of weeping.[13] We are struck by the poet's ability to make a personal theme yield a general meaning, much like the African dirge singer on a mission of communal purgation of negative emotions.

In *Naked Testimonies* the poet overcomes the mournful perplexity of broken truces with studied, deliberate, renunciation of all that discredit the villainous subjects of her mournful sorrows. While adopting a sombre, semi-elegaic tone:

> I tell a tale of sour tangerines
> And shrivelled penises
> In the furnace of testicle crushers
> Diamonds are mere stones
> In the trauma of dry sentences ...

---

[13]Toyin Adewale *Naked Testimonies* Mace, Lagos 1995 (Acknowledgement)

This tale of 'sour tangerines' signifying ruined hopes, as of death, is further extrapolated in images of ruin and desolation:

> ...
> Hearths crumble
> in courtyards of ruin
> Absurd altars say I am sacrifice...

Tragic losses whirl along into its third and fourth sequences, unearthing more benumbing spectres, until entering the fifth movement where the poet unravels a visionary triumph. It is also an emotional and psychological triumph. In spite of all human tribulations, (wo)man stands firm and resolute:

> Striding upon my high places
> Shield my voice
> I walk in fire

There is a cold cynical stance typical of Adewale's poetry which strives to belie the depth of the hurt residing within.

> ...
> scowls that decrease our face value
> This is the night
> ...

> vigil of septic pits
> This is the storm
> ...
> solid sheet of shattered eggs

Loss and disappointment are ideas that run through most of the poems in *Naked Testimonies*. This symbolic loss, very much like that of a cherished dream, has the power of creating a new awareness in the individual. With this awareness comes faith in the self. As the poet says:

> There are lacerations
> But we shall salve our wounds
> Calm sandstorms...

The poetic gift of optimism is neither squandered nor inured
> ...on the trail/of light
> ...
> soaring and prideful like an eagle in flight
>
> ('Fresh Dawns')

It is rather enhanced by the promise of eternal kind. Thus in 'Untitled' we have,

> hope (that) flutters
> ...

> Like a quaking foundation

Adewale's poetry subtly leads into deeper knowingness and awareness that prod mere human sentiments and emotions into the realm of indomitable spirit.

> ...
> I'll hold your sure word
> Knowing it's spirit and blood.

Areas of Artistic Convergence

The poetry of Aiyejina, Osundare, Adewale and Chin Ce, acting from the influence of their times and age, succeed in exploring the range of emotions to delineate the near tragic complexities of their society. They have employed these varying elegiac emotions in their inward and outward creative outlets without hindrance. This marks the dawn of a new kind of poetic or creative liberty in serious African writing now and probably in later years to come.

The present world of poets of the third generation reflects strong cultural sensibility. 'Unfolding Season,' is full of traditional imagery drawn from the agrarian landscape where the major occupation is farming. Before the seeds are planted, the land is burnt and later cleared. The poet captures this action as his imagery in the following poem.

> the smoke of burning bush ...
> antelopes and grass-cutters
> scuttling out of the flames

Another way in which these poets celebrate their cultural environment is by the inculcation of religious practices or local occupation in their poetry. For example, Niyi Osundare's 'Cloud Watching' is poetry in celebration of the pastoral life. Prominent in the style of modern African poetry is the use of the 'rich imagery of the African environment ...unstifled by far-fetched allusions'[14] The poems are replete with 'storm-ravaged banana leaves,' 'like the epidemic laden-noon heat,' also 'fireflies,' 'soldier ants,' 'like greying creepers on dying trees.'[15] etc. There are attempts to retain the reality of local flora and fauna:

> 'Skins scaly like iguana's,' 'feet swollen
> like water melon.'[16]

Drawn from local environment to bring vivid pictures to the mind's eye, these images serve to validate the varied experiences of both poet and audience.

A further point of artistic convergence among these poets is the use of simple language, as against the convoluted

---

[14] Ezenwa Ohaeto, 'Aiyejina and Ojaide: Two Threnodic Poets,' *The Guardian*, Saturday, August 9, 1986, p.13

[15] Funso Aiyejina, 1984, p.23

[16] Niyi Osundare, 1983, p.7

diction of the previous generation. This may be an attempt to make their art accessible to the people whose experiences they seek to register. Of striking interest in this convergence is the incidence of common connotations and symbolisms. Funso Aiyejina's use of predatory images like 'dog,' 'snake,' and 'eagle,' in describing Nigerian leaders reappear in the laments of Chin Ce and Ohaeto. Niyi Osundare and Funso Aiyejina use 'soldier ants' as metaphors for oppression.

The language of the new threnodists is also characterised by frequent code-switching where local nomenclatures are used in formal English. Here, names like '*tanwiji*,' '*molue*,' '*danfo*,' and '*dagbere*,' abound in Osundare as a matter of conscious artistry. In Aiyejina Yoruba and Hausa phrases are virtually transported into the poem. In 'The year of Hopeless hope' the lines '*lai lai Alamu O le dede la eewo Orisa*' express the Yoruba thought that 'nothing happens from nothing' in a manner that retains the collective belief in that truism where its English equivalent could not have sufficed. From Ce's poems, we have '*Dodan*,' '*agbada*,' '*menini*,' '*surugede*,' retaining their cultural trappings in spite of the formality of his English idioms. Aiyejina plays with syntax and morphemes of the language, breaking words into segments in order to achieve pun and ambiguity. In 'The year of a hopeless hope,' linguistic truncations: 'Of/f course,' 'con/tract/or' imbue the poem with levels of meaning. We are struck sometimes by how Osundare manipulates words to create rhythm and rhyme. Copious use of allophones, alliterations and assonance abound in his art. In 'Siren,' 'buntings and banners ... brazen bombasts...' call to mind the festive mood that our depressed cities are made to wear when the 'big shots' come to town. Alliterations and assonance 'begging bickering,' 'clangourous convoy,' 'acrobats and motor bikes,' render a sense of rhythm and motion to his poetry.

Most poignant in the poetry of Adewale and Chin Ce are some ethereal images. Recurrent images denoting the elements: fire, waves, water, wind, clouds, light and nature: 'hills,' 'waterfall,' 'mountain paths,' 'sands,' 'sun,' 'moon' flow through their writings. Adewale and Chin Ce make no deliberate attempt to speak in the traditional high flown proverbial language and imagery remarkable of their contemporaries. But this is not to say that the language of these two poets does not reflect local environment. There is rather a preponderance of images mirroring urban settings -- influences that have come to be accepted as a part of emerging African societies with which they are more accustomed. For example, Adewale's 'jigsaw puzzles,' 'Gethsamane,' 'diesel,' 'knife,' 'spoon,' 'fork,' 'peak,' 'cap,' 'car,' 'tarmac,' and 'sunglasses,' amplify the urban culture. In his second collection, *Full Moon*, Chin Ce's poetic landscape is replete with 'polythene,' 'jazz,' 'siren snouts,' 'ships,' 'revolution,' 'doctrines,' 'sentry,' and 'missiles.' In style and technique Chin Ce's profuse deployment of alliterations and assonance,

> Passions potted with pomp...
> ...
> Scream / against your yeoman's yoke...
> ...
> Prints in sinking sands ...
>
> Greed grabbed the gritty mask
> For prize fight at Vanity Fair...
>
> Strut and fluff
> Feathers in the gathering clouds ...
>
> Prattled their practised hands

for the effect of scorn or ribaldry, is almost reminiscent of the 'age of reason' in western poetry,[17] that era in English verse which witnessed works of satire against social and political anomalies more than any other period in English literary history. Strictly speaking, Africa has produced leaders who rank among the mediaeval lords of Europe in stupidity and

---

[17] Anthony Thwaite *Six Centuries of Verse* Thames Methuen (Introduction)

bestiality. For the enlightened artist, therefore, the unfettered choice of diction that may allow a fair representation of those transient realities becomes the true index of art in touch with its times.

Figure 1 The 'total' African Dirge

```
                    Ancestral
    Abuse            Realm              Praise
         \                                  /
          \          Death                 /
           \                              /
        Aggressor                      Victim
     N                                      P
             \                          /
              Villain              Hero
                    _____/
                           |
                        Mourner
Level 1
                     Burial/Funeral  ←———— Occasion

Level 2
                      Choral/Solo
                           |
                         Death  ←———— Theme

                     Journey/Search  ←———— Motifs

                    Varying moods
         Despair —— of the dirge ——  Elation
            |                           |
        Frustration                  Triumph
            |                           |
          Anger                      Laughter
            |                           |
           Loss                      Discovery
            |                           |
           Dark                        Light
```

Chapter 6

A Theory of the African Dirge

*The dialectical framework for African dirge performance
*A dirge locution *Western patterns and African structures*

Dialectical Framework

It is a matter of tradition that the mourner has come to occupy an important position in African funerals. Our dialectical framework for the African dirge therefore underscores the importance of traditional performance in Africa where the mourner functions within a definite occasion of transition, burial, or during a funeral any of which may inspire his creative vision.

The first level provides a dialectical framework for understanding the dirge performance. Polarised on L, the Negative plank, is the villain and aggressor, personified by death and extended to include all man-made and natural circumstances that cause pain and loss to man. These include war, poisoning, accidents, earthquakes, epidemics, and failed dreams, broken relationships and human disappointments. On them are rained the traditional vilification reserved for those responsible for the death of a loved one.

On the right of the positive plank (L) is the hero-victim, the deceased whose demise inspires the mourner's poetry. These include historical figures or such themes as Okigbo, Cabral, Mathi Kulersegaram, Bala'nku, Nweke, Nigeria's dream of good leadership, national unity and others. Following these are the sympathisers who may be family members of the deceased or his colleagues such as Obiechina, Egudu, Nwoga, Ekwensi, Achebe, Soyinka, Clark, Ogbalu, etc, in Chimezie's dirge on Okigbo. All the praises lavished on the deceased are shared in part by the sympathisers who are mutually linked by a common fraternal or intellectual cause. Death, as sub-deity, looms above these and beyond includes the unknown where dwell the ancestors who departed long ago.

Within the second level (2), the actual dirge in performance is realised in the two kinds of African dirge we have noted as solo and choral, both which concentrate on the major theme of death and tragedy. Death is most often expressed in traditional motifs of journey and search. While also expressed through other range of imagery available to the poet, they elicit the general mood that splits into the positive (R) and negative (L).

Negatively, we have feelings of despair, frustration, anger, loss and varying nuances of dark fate. Positively, elation, triumph, laughter, humour and the subliminal feelings come with the discovery or realisation of truth which dawning upon the poet his consciousness is illuminated and he is brought to the light of new understanding.

This in its compact graphic presentation forms a descriptive framework for interpreting the dirge in Africa. A single dirge rendition may, no doubt, be unable to express all the features listed. In fact individual poems may touch on few aspects. We can say that the fully realised African dirge poetry has all or most of the features of 1 and 2. The most recent individual poems have witnessed forms of western dirge which are similar in part, and also mostly dissimilar to the traditional features.

In the first category, we have the traditionals such as 'Anyi-na-acho,' 'Onuma,' 'Mbem mmuo,' 'Iwe,' 'Okigbo ebelebe egbuole.' For the second part there are 'Song for the Seer,' 'Lament in a storm,' 'The Story of a Ceylonese Girl' and

'Lament for the dauntless Three.'

'Lament in a Storm' largely falls under the structural framework of level 1.

The mood of tragedy dominates the entire superstructure. It is full of grief and sorrow thereby expousing the Negative plank with 'sadness,' 'sorrow,' 'sighing,' 'bitterness,' 'gasping (of breath),' and 'throbbing (of heart).' The greater focus on Okigbo emphasises noble qualities such 'soldier,' 'martyr,' 'saint,' and 'cathedral column.'

From the overt vilification of death and his killers, the poet's memory also incorporates other enduring positive experiences of the deceased who 'slept in fresh/lavender scented streets,' 'bathed in perfumed waters,' 'had three thousand devoted servants,' and 'threaded bosomed garlands/of yellow and orange flowers.'

Other dirges may go beyond this to invoke the spirit of the dead, give it suggestions or make postulates as to future actions expected of it. In this case, the mourner in his position at the centre of the whole action would have moved upward, so to speak, bypassing both positive and negative emotional attitudes into the unknown where dwells the spirit of the dead. This direct access into the spiritual realm is often common among the aged bards.

Normally, the bard walks in at the burial to enact his poetic rendition in the form of a proclamation similar to the following.

>Nwanne, Nwanne
>I lawa la!
>I lawa la ye-o
>Naa nti n'ife m na-agwa gi
>Ya buru nwoke
>Ya buru nwanyi
>Mere gi ihe-a
>Asim gi
>Ya buru nwata
>Ya buru nwata
>Ya buru oke' yi
>Ruru ala-a
>Ekwele ya hie ura
>Che ya ura-o
>Ya iyi-o
>Che ya nku-o
>Che ya umu-o
>Ekwela ya noo abali asaa taaa![1]
>(Umuahia 1992)

>My sister, my sister
>Are you gone?

---

[1] Rendition at a funeral ceremony witnessed by the author, Umuahia, 1992. (Translation by the author)

> Are you really gone?
> Listen to what I tell you
> If it was man
> If it was woman
> That did this to you
> I tell you
> If it was a child
> If it was an adult
> That committed this crime
> Never let him sleep
> Never let him fetch water
> Never let him fetch firewood
> Do not let him to see his children
> Do not let him last seven days

A composition parallel to this invocation to the dead-in-the-unknown could be found in this excerpt from K. A. Ude's 'To B.U.'

> Barth
> You abandoned your bath
> And swam in sweat
> In a society that hates sweat
>
> Barth
> You abandoned your brothers
> And offended your friends
> For a community that cast you out
> In need

> ...
> Nothing has changed
> But before you come again
> Understand the dance
> The dance you did not understand [2]

The poem is a tribute to a friend who died in the course of duty. At the workplace Barth had worked so hard and had no value for relatives. At death, however, it was his brothers, sisters and friends that camel. The people whom he worked for had no time to come and find out what had happened. They cited official procedures and bureaucratic bottlenecks. In view of this, all the deceased's sacrifice appeared to be in vain. The poet achieves the effect of this invocation by directly addressing the deceased and calling him in the second and third stanzas of the poem:

> Barth
> You abandoned your bath
> ...

> Barth
> You abandoned your brothers
> And offended your friends
> ...

The above dirge poems address the soul of the dead.

---

[2] K.A. Ude, 'For Bartholomew B.U' in *Smiling Through Tears*, Abuja, Pecand Publishers Ltd, 1997, p. 68

The first is a call for vengeance. The dead is invoked to take on different forms of vengeance on those who caused his death. The second poem goes further to outline expectations the mourner has for the deceased:

> ... before you come again
> Understand the dance
> The dance you did not understand

This symbolic dance is the art of survival, of common communal values which, sadly, is no longer comprehensible to many westernised Africans –those like Bartholomew Nwafor. The mood sad, melancholic and bitter is probably due to the expressed sentiment of double tragedy: that of Barth's death and the treachery of his colleagues after the fact.

The poet-mourner has transcended the intermediary stages between him and the unknown ancestral regions, the metaphysical world of deities. Its mood does not, therefore, dilate between the opposing emotional states of negative and positive. Nor is he encumbered by a pondering journey and search for the deceased.

What is emphasised is the communication that is evoked, like a chant, from the living to the dead. Pol Ndu also achieves this effect in part rather than the whole of his poem 'Song for Seer.'

> Come back to this void
> Seed of seeing and knowing
> Razor-tongued weaver-bird...

The poet demonstrates that the mourner would often exploit the range of the structure of the dirge in Africa to create varying effects of the subliminal or mystical.

> Come among mortal
> Immortal Man
> Move around your flicker...[3]

So far in this study if there lies a rounded exploitation of the whole range of the dirge structure, we must look for this in the poem of Emeka Chimezie whose dirge poem has been illustrated under the graphic (Figure 1) framework.

Western patterns and African structures

Some of the structures of Western dirge can be contrasted with the traditional African dirge structure. The poem 'For Christopher Okigbo' by Wole Soyinka is the model of English tradition of poetry, written in traditional couplet.

---

[3] Pol Ndu, p. 35

> Perhaps 'tis kinder that vultures toil
> To cleanse torch-bearers for the soil [4]

The mood is withdrawn and sombre, meditative and philosophical. The opening statement is a proposition of options, introduced regularly with the repetition of 'kinder.'

> (a) Kinder that vultures toil
> To cleanse torch-bearers for the soil
>
> (b) Kinder that dying eyes should close
> To truths of light on weed and rose...
>
> (c) Kinder indeed full reckoning paid
> A circle closed, a lowered shade
>
> (d) Kinder that, lured by cleansing rites
> He fell, burnt offering on the heights

Each of the propositions is followed by a rejection, the 'deproposition,' introduced with 'than'

> (a) than eagles bare their living bone
> Chained to an eternity of stone
>
> (b) than read in their own live entrails
> Fulfilment of the web of nails

---

[4] Achebe and Okafor, 1978, p. 42

(c)   ...than a spirit seared
    In violated visions and truths
        inured

By this method, the poetry projects some solace in dark fate. The poet interprets death as an act of sacrifice 'burnt offering on the heights' even if a misguided one 'lured by cleansing rites.'

The 'torch' of Okigbo's verse would 'waken mountain shines fused to an alien tuber of mines!' His boundless thoughts 'would climb the wings of time.' There is seen albeit vaguely, a nobility of sacrifice (such as poet taking up arms) compared to the shame of cowardice. Because of the role of Okigbo as 'burnt offering' his stature becomes that of 'eternal provender for time.'

The poet is not given to effusive expressions of sorrow or demand for vengeance. There are neither prevalent impulses nor motifs of search or journey. There cannot be found in this poem an overt address to the soul of the dead hero as in Ude's 'Nwafor' or Ndu's 'Song for Seers.' The experience communicated in the poem is a private one. The communality of traditional dirge aesthetics is distant. As a dirge, its aesthetics lean to the English tradition.

Comparatively, Soyinka's poem for Okigbo affirms

the poet's triumph over death, much as is elaborated by Dylan Thomas.

> ... death shall have no dominion
> Dead men naked they shall be one
> With the man in the wind and the west moon
> When their bones are picked clean and
> The cleaned bones gone.
> They shall have stars at elbow and foot
> Though they go mad they shall be sane
> Though they sink through the sea, they
> Shall rise again
> Though lives be lost love shall not
> And death shall have no dominion [5]

Thomas elaborates upon Christian images of resurrection, and of the prophetic bones that shall rise again in the books of Ezekiel and Revelation. It is the moment of resurrection and ascension where all defects are cured and the dead become new celestial beings with 'stars at elbow and foot.' Death is quashed in this order.

But this is not to say that in Western aesthetics there are no series of praises for the dead. In the poem of Laurence Durrell to a medieval crusader, praises read like an epitaph at the graveside as the title of the poem and its opening lines denote.

---

[5] John Waine ed., *Anthology of Modern Poetry,* Hutchinson Press, London, 1963, p.30

> Here lies Michael of the small bone
> The pride of the lion is gone home
> God lend England such a one[6]

Sometimes in this oratory, the mood can be almost comical despite its dominantly introverted Christian themes.

> A knight's memoriam is only love
> So Michael with his dog in his leg
> To his sweet vicar is gone above

There is the hint of victory in the line at the end of the poem:

> Michael the Englishmen of the small bone
> Simple and pure as water in a spoon
> God lend our England such a one

which is a recapitulation of the beginning stanza in the five-stanza poetry. Michael had a breath 'as pure as the great dew of may' and 'spoke to God with the tongue of great bell.'

Such descriptions are typical of English funeral orations and give Western dirge poetry a distinct sombre restraint of tone and heaviness of mood. The weather is also an important aspect of English dirge poetry, much as in an Englishman's conversations. Nature mourns with the poet the loss of the loved one, enforcing in the sensitivity, the elements of darkness and dejection, as can be seen in W.H Auden:

---

[6] John Waine ed., 1963, p.167

> He disappeared in the dead of winter
> The brooks were frozen, the airports almost deserted,
> And snow disfigured the public statues;
> The mercury sank in the mouth of the dying day
> O all the instruments agree
> The day of his death was a dark cold day.[7]

In 'A young Greek killed in the War,' this poet goes on to describe the tyranny of death, its imposition of the tragic gloom in the minds of men even despite the clemency and harmony of nature.

> When music comes upon the airs of spring
> Faith fevers the blood; counter to harmony
> Melancholy moves, preservatory and predatory[8]

At the beginning stanza, he had sketched the death of the young soldier in the image of war.

> They dug a trench and threw him in the grave
> Shallow as youth; and poured the wine out
> Soaking the tunic and the dry Attic air
> They covered him lightly and left him there

Both language and scenery depict war haste. War, the voracious man-eater has reduced life to a short, brusque, and meaningless equation. English tradition thereby seeks to

---

[7] Anthony Thwaite, 1984, p. 231

[8] John Waine ed., 1963 p. 143

preserve the identity of the deceased through the verse, through the voice of the bard. In the last lines, Eberhart writes:

> The light is a container of treachery
> The light is preserver of pantheon
> The light is lost from that young eye
> Hearing music, I speak, lest he should die.[9]

The dirge becomes the monument and reminder of life. It furnishes the community a creative means of overcoming the fear of death. It thereby serves a social need, more significantly, a psychological release from the fear and depression of loss.

It has been observed that the African dirge goes beyond this psychology. Out of the despondency of tragedy and separation, there is no final loss. The poetic consciousness holds the possibility of movement beyond the mortal, and into the ancestral realm. This is often demonstrated by direct dialogue with the departed.

> Rise Chris
> Expound Chris
> Then stay awhile brother.[10]

---

[9] John Waine ed., 1963 p. 143
[10] Chinua Achebe and Dubem Okafor ed., 1978, p.20

The departed soul appears to be in control of its own destiny. It has the choice of coming back to the land of men in another incarnation it will choose to continue the work yet unfinished. The ontological view of the world thrives in African dirge where the poet demonstrates this deep awareness of his society, beliefs and tradition.

It is here that the total African dirge emerges, exploiting the occasion of tragedy and loss in rites and transition ceremonies. Alone, or with the choral participators, the mourner searches for the beloved around familiar terrains often traversing the land of the dead in his mystical journeys while running through the gamut of human emotions, positive or negative.

It is very much like warfare in itself, with death and its agents poised on the opposing flank, and the deceased, poet-mourner with his sympathisers on the righteous heroic side. They take the praises and throw the blames at the opponents. Thus is the passage marked, until leading to the realms of the unknown, the ancestral abode. From there, the dialogue may continue if the poet is a seer too, to yield finally into the mystic dimensions where the immortals share the stage with mortals in a continuing tradition of spirito-material interactions.

Figure 3 shows the mourner of Odogwu Kabral

(Amilca Cabral) in such state of solemn grief as furnishes the occasion for most successful African dirge poetry. As in Nwosu's 'Lament,' the focus is on the dead victim, Amilca Cabral, whose sterling qualities appear to have been eviscerated by the might of death. Consequently the tragic victims are both himself and the land of Africa by extension. As a solo dirge, its reflective qualities, as expected, lead to a sense of triumph. The bard even bids the dead hero a fraternal farewell 'Odogwu Kabral n'odu mma.' (Great Cabral, fare thee well)

The structure of this dirge framework has taken on the binary lamentation structure. This could, in extension to the laments of the latter poets, achieve an overall amplification that would prove quite advancing and illuminating. In Adewale's 'Thawing,' for example, the theme of separation enlivens a somewhat 'threnodic essence' in its powerfully illustrative graph of separation and rejection culminating in a change in consciousness. It is hardly of importance that the theme is not directly on physical death for the demise of love and cherished dreams is not inextricably or perfectly exclusive of the tragedy of mortality. Both denote a physical separation, a permanent atrophy, a parting of ways, perhaps not as with that dreadful feeling of ultimate finality with the one as with the other.

Every journey shall, in communal world view, end in a triumph of some sorts. Our ('she') heroine in this mourning holds out superior moral qualities where the villain 'once magnificent' is now 'diminished.' Mockery and contempt of the villain lead us to the conclusive ending of this solo song, relieves us of the 'thawing.'

In contrast, Chin Ce's 'Eclipse' shows profuse deployment of abuse and expletives. This means the hero villain divide is strongly tilted to the Negative (R) in its mournful deploration of a failing nationhood. This Negative polarity has in its cluster such emotions as contempt, vilification, abuse, hectoring, indignation and even satirical humour.

The 'Eclipse' scenario may be thus illustrated: Dressed as the rapacious death itself, the African president presides over his minions: politicians ('loyal dogs') and instruments of repression, who combine to visit poverty and deprivation on their people. Unlike in the secular limitations of his contemporary, the poet's satire goes further into an enunciation of the apocalyptic.

This technique, likeable to a peep into the unknown

ancestral realms, is reminiscent of the total dirge poetry of Emeka Chimezie in 'Okigbo Ebelebe Egbuole.' But here, it comes like prophecy –the poet as seer in the literary culture of Africa. 'Time' recurs quite frequently, the third and significant force, the unknown arm in the triangle of human interactions in a world of human limitations and cosmic possibilities. In the futility of presidential chicanery, the masses are to enjoy a solstice with the revolutionary upheaval of powers.

There is no gainsaying the fact that further explorations into the dirge structure using the foregoing illustrations are possible frameworks for further stylistic interpretation of African dirge poetry and the African aesthetics. With this trend may also come a more complete realisation of art among the bards in their practice of blending culture and artistry to the poetics of modern dirge expressions.

Fig. 2 Dirge Structure of '*Lament in a Storm*'

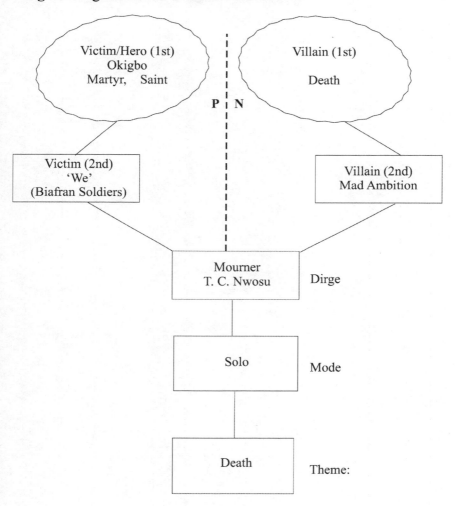

Fig. 3: Dirge Structure of '*Odogwu Kabral*'

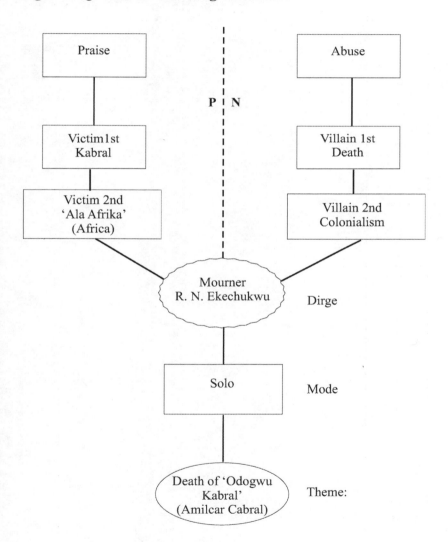

Chapter 7

Summary

Different dirge compositions and dirge sentiments in Africa have been explored in this book. These include the oral, written and those of English expressions.

A historical overview corroborates the idea that despite the geographical expanse of the African continent, most of its cultural traditions are essentially uniform. This has therefore informed the particularisation of this study on the southern belt of Nigeria and a few other poetry of sub-Saharan Africa as representative of the dirge tradition in Africa.

Incidentally, the death in the Nigerian civil war of Christopher Okigbo, whose tragedy inspired probably the most singular wealth of poetry from all over the world, provides a uniform theme for some of the poems studied in this book. The choice of a common theme has helped to identify and highlight the distinct stylistic features of individual poets.

Generally, any event of death gives rise to the

composition of dirges and their oral renditions. The occasion is always either burial, memorial or funeral ceremonies. We have come to appreciate the position of the performer who is almost the poet-mourner at all times.

Two major categories of traditional African dirges have been identified: the solo individual dirges like 'Onye Nzoputa,' 'Onuma,' which are often composed for particular persons. The other category is the popular or choral dirges like 'Anyi na-acho,' 'Iwe,' etc, which can be adapted to any burial situation just like Chinua Achebe does in 'Uno Onwu Okigbo.'

The major differences in these two kinds of dirges lie not so much in formal structures as in elegiac tone and mood. Whereas one, popular, is always short, light hearted and communal in both ownership and presentation, the other is dense, sombre, and highly amenable to individual artistry.

Other dirges (written both in Igbo and English languages) exhibit characteristics of either of these two categories of traditional dirges. Thus the poems of Chinua Achebe, Emeka Chimezie, R. M. Ekechukwu, (of Igbo Language expression), and Pol Ndu, Ossie Enekwe, T.C. Nwosu and Chinweizu (of English Langauge expression) borrow immensely from the formal structures, tone, mood and range of imagery from the traditional African dirge and milieu.

The difference therefore lies, not in the process of transmission as such, nor the language of rendition, but the variables of composition by individual poet artistes. For instance, whereas Emeka Chimezie and Ossie Enekwe exploit the choral mode of dirge rendition, T.C Nwosu and R.M Ekechukwu prefer the solo composition. Pol Ndu, on the other hand, finds it better to mourn through the mystic concourse of seer imagination.

It has rightly been stated that these poets Emeka Chimezie, Chinua Achebe, R. M. Ekechukwu, Pol Ndu, T. C. Nwosu, Chinweizu and Ossie Enekwe by their writing succeed in producing lasting testaments to an enduring poetic tradition. They therefore meet the challenge of expressing contemporary themes and projecting personal feelings in a voice at home with their culture and tradition.

Perhaps the employment of African dirge styles in modern poetry will come to be appreciated in fuller detail when literary critics begin to look deeper into the new poetry of Funso Aiyejina, Niyi Osundare, Chin Ce and Toyin Adewale. The threnodic world (in the poetry) of the former and the sombre semi-elegaic tones of the latter reveal a quality of modern African art which is at once distanced from contrivance of art (domestication) and yet environmentally honed to the communal landscape. A study of this departure is necessary to elicit the various nuances in style of presentation and uniqueness of form.

Finally, we have propounded a theory for the African dirge which situates the mourner in the middle of the dirge sentiment. Using the occasions of funeral, burial, or transition, he composes his songs (whether solo or choral) in honour of the deceased and for the enjoyment and upliftment of the audience. He explores all the negative and positive sentiments in the process of composition and rendition. Death and all agents of distraction are villains, while the deceased, the mourner, and his hoard of sympathisers are the victims/heroes.

The mood also varies from that of Positive (elation, triumph, laughter, etc) to Negative (despair, frustration, anger, loss etc). At other times, the bard transcends the terrestrial universe to that of the abode of the ancestors where he communicates directly with the deceased. All these form the artistic corollaries of African dirge poetry as distinct from Western poetry which is primarily individualistic and seeks often to preserve the identity of the deceased in epitaphs. Western dirge tradition has been found to serve a purely psychological function with its heavy Christian innuendoes, while the African dirge on the other hand, seeks to perpetuate the continuity of life beyond the natural mortality of the flesh. All loss is never total, for, as the African animist tradition goes, there is always the undying hope of another rebirth.

Select Bibliography

Achebe Chinua. *Morning Yet on Creation Day*, Heinemann Educational Books: London 1972

— — —. *The Trouble with Nigeria*, Fourth Dimension Publishers: Enugu 1985

Achebe C. and Okafor D. *Don't Let Him Die*, Fourth Dimensions Publishers: Enugu 1978.

Adewale, Toyin. *Naked Testimonies*, Mace Books: Lagos 1995.

Ajayi, J.F.A. *Christian Missions in Nigeria 1841-1891* Longman: London 1965.

Anozie, S. O. *Christopher Okigbo* Africana Publishing Corporation: U.S.A. 1972.

Arnold, Alan. *Young Sherlock Holmes*. Paramount pictures Corporation, New York, 1985

Awoonor, Kofi. *The Breast of the Earth*, Nok Publishers International: New York 1975.

Ce, Chin. *An African Eclipse*, Handel Books: Enugu 2001.

Chimezie, Emeka 'Igbo War Poetry,' International Seminar on Igbo Literature, the Society for the Promotion of Igbo Language and Culture, (SPILC), University of Nigeria Nsukka, 12-15 August, 1981.

Chinweizu. *Voices from Twentieth Century Africa,* Faber and Faber: London 1988.

— — —. *Energy Crisis and other Poems* NOK Publishers: Lagos 1978.

Chinweizu, Jemie, O. and Madubuike I. *Toward the Decolonisation of African Literature,* Fourth Dimension Publishers: Enugu. 1980.

Davids, P. K. *Igbo Naming and Age-Grading*, Handel Books: Enugu 1989.

Davidson, Basil. *The Black Man's Burden: Africa and the Curse of the Nation State*, Spectrum Books: Ibadan 2000.

Drachler, Jacob. *African Heritage.* Collier Books: New York 1964.

Egudu, R. N. and Nwoga, D. I. [Eds.] *Poetic Heritage: Igbo Traditional Verse.* Heinemann Educational Books: London 1973.

Ekechukwu, R.M. 'Odogwu Kabral n'odu mma', in *Akpa Uche, an Anthology of Igbo Poems*, Oxford University Press: Ibadan 1975.

Emenyonu, E. N. *The Rise of the Igbo Novel,* Oxford University Press: Ibadan 1978.

— — — .[Ed.] *Critical Theory and African Literature,* Heinemann Educational: Ibadan 1987.

Enekwe, Ossie. *Broken Pots,* Greenfield Review Press: New York 1977.

Finnegan Ruth. *Oral Literature in Africa,* Oxford University Press: Nairobi 1970.

— — —. *Oral Poetry*, Cambridge University Press: London 1977

Hayward, John ed. *Selected Prose: T.S Eliot*, Penguin Books

Ltd: Victoria 1963.

Heywood, Christopher. [Ed.] *Perspectives on African Literature,* Heinemann Educational Books: London 1971.

Jones, Eldred Ed. *African Literature Today* No 6. Heinemann Educational: London 1972.

— — —. *African Literature Today* No 10. Heinemann Educational: London 1979.

Ndu, Pol. *Songs for Seers*, NOK Publishers: New York 1974.

Nwoga, D. I. [Ed.] *West African Verse*, Longman Group Limited: United Kingdom 1982.

— — —. [Ed.] *Perspectives on Okigbo*, Three Continents Press: Washington D.C. 1984.

Okigbo, Christopher. *Labyrinths* Africana Publishing Corporation: U.S.A. 1971.

Ogbalu, F. C. *Abu Igbo*, Merit Standard Press: Onitsha 1974.

Thwaite, Anthony. *Six Centuries of Verse*, Methuen: London. 1984.

Ude, K. A. *Smiling Through Tears*, Pecand Publishers: Abuja 1997.

Vincent, Theo. *Black and African Writing*, Emacoprint: Lagos 1981.

Von Daniken, Erich. *In Search of Ancient Gods*, Souvenir Press: Great Britain 1974.

— — —. *Chariots of the Gods? Was God an astronaut?* Corgi Books: London, 1980.

Waine, John. [Ed.] *Anthology of Modern Poetry*, Hutchinson Press: London 1985.

Zahar, Renate. *Colonialism and Alienation*, Ethiope Publishing: Benin City 1974.

Index

A

A Farewell. See Chin Ce
A Letter to Lynda and other Poems. See Funso Aiyejina
Achebe, 137, 152, 176, 177
Adewale, 125, 140, 143, 146, 167, 177
Aesop. See Ethiope
aesthetic
  dirge, 161
  western, 162
African
  dirge, 149, 166
  dirge poetry, 168
  funeral, 149
  philosophy, 5
  poetic heritage, 21
  poetics, 132, 169
  poetry, 124, 126, 131, 133
  sensibility, 140, 143, 169
African-American, 113
Afro- and Euro-centricism, 90
Aiyejina, 125, 128, 130, 132
alliterations, 146, 147
animism, 3
Aristotle, 12
Armattoe, 12
Aryan
  ideology, 12

Auden
　W. H., 163

B
Before the dawn dawns. See Funso Aiyejina
Biafra, 63, 66, 79, 103, 109, 110, 111
black man, 12
Book of the Dead, 5

C
capitalism, 12
Casely-Hayford, 12
Ce. See Chin Ce
Ceylonese Girl, 110, 111, 112
Chin Ce 125, 132, 177
Chinua. See Achebe
Chinweizu, 125, 176, 177
Christian
　themes, 163
Christopher Okigbo, 175
Chukwuma Nzeogwu, 119
Clark
　J. P., 67, 70
Cloud Watching, 144
code switching, 145
cognition, 122
commitment, 12

concept
  of Death, 1
Congo, 8
consciousness, 94, 97, 118
contemporaneity, 13
corruption, 12
cross-
  cultural influences, 90
  cross-culturalisation, 3
cultural
  unity of Africa, 1

D

dark fate, 153
darkness, 163
David Diop, 12
dead-in-the-unknown, 155
dearth, 127
Dei-Anang, 12
Dennis Brutus, 12
Dennis Osadebay, 12
deproposition, 159
dirge
  structure, 166, 168, 169
domestication, 178
Dylan Thomas, 162

E

Eberhart
  Richard, 163
Eclipse, 132, 133, 134, 136, 137
Egudu, 11, 152
Egypt, 5
Ekwensi, 80
Emeka Chimezie, 82
Enekwe, 176, 177
Energy Crisis. See Chinweizu
English, 91, 93, 98, 99, 103
Englishman, 163
experimental poetry, 117
Ezenwa Ohaeto, 124

F

framework
  for interpreting dirge, 152
Fuff, 138
Full Moon, 147
Funso Aiyejina. See Aiyejina

G

Ghana, 7
Greece, 11

H
Horus, 5

I
Igbo lament, 119
immortals, 94
incarnation, 166
inflation, 126
Invocation, 156, 157
Invocations and Admonitions, 118
Ismail B. Garba, 125

J
Jacob Drachler, 14, 17
J.P Ajayi, 15
Jeremiah, 125

L
L.S Senghor, 11
lament, 124, 132, 139
   for the Dauntless Three, 117, 118, 119
   in a Storm. See T.C Nwosu
loss
  feeling of, 108
  after-loss, 123

M

Martels, 9
Mathi Kulersegaram, 109
Merveille Herskovits, 13
modern African poetry, 11
Modest Proposal. See Jonathan Swift
mourner, 18, 21, 30, 59, 79
Murtala Mohammed, 118
mythic role, 118
mythology, 108

N

Naked Testimonies. See Toyin Adewale
Ndu
　Pol, 91, 156, 159
Negritude, 12
new experimentation, 122
Nigerian
　national history, 119
Niyi Osundare. See Osundare
Nwoga, 72, 73, 80
Nwosu
　T. C., 101

O

Obiechina, 72, 73, 80
Odogwu Kabral, 83, 86
Oduduwa myth, 2

Ofo
　chant, 98
Ogbalu
　Mazi, 67, 70
Ogu eri dike, 125
Okigbo, 60, 61
Okigbo
　ebelebe egbuole, 59
　uno onwu, 37, 60
ontological world-view, 4
Ossie Enekwe. See Enekwe

P

parallelism
　lexical, 107
　structural, 101
　syntactic, 105
perfumed waters, 106
poetic evocation, 117
poetic universe, 106
Pol Ndu. See Ndu

R

R. N. Egudu, 150
Rithmetic of Ruse. See Niyi Osundare

S

satire

Chin, 168
Satyagraha, 107, 109
Song for Seer. See Pol Ndu
Soyinka, Wole, 159
stylistic
  highlighting, 77
  intertextuality, 90
sun god. See Horus
symbolic, 7, 37
syntactic parallels, 101

T

T. S. Eliot, 124
T.C Nwosu. See Nwosu
The Story of a Ceylonese Girl. See Enekwe
The year of hopeless-hope. See Funso Aiyejina
total
  content, 121
  loss, 134
Toyin Adewale. See Adewale
tragedy, 116, 117, 120, 73
tragic
  choice, 114
  complexities, 143
  destiny, 114
  gloom, 164
  loss, 141
  victims, 167

voice
 threnodic, 124, 127

W
Western
 patterns, 159
 poetry, 163
Wind and Storm, 137

Y
Yeats, 137

By the same author...

New Voices: A Collection of Recent Poetry from Nigeria
GMT Emezue [Ed.]

This simple compendium of recent poetry from Nigeria contains some of the most remarkable breaths of creative energy to come from this side of black Africa. The poems from over fifty young contributors have been compiled and edited for not only the reading enjoyment of the public but also, and more significantly, to fan the creative embers latent in the new generation of creative artistes from Nigeria.

Journal of New Nigerian Poetry NNP No. 2
GMT Emezue [Ed.]

Read some current critical perspectives on Nigeria poetry. This seminal criticism of African poetry by rising voices in critical studies in Nigeria, will help to chart new trends in recent poetry in English.

The writers also compare two generations of Nigerian poets, including what has been dubbed the inter- and intra personal concourse of the new poetics. For those interested in new Nigerian poetry, this addition to criticism of poetry becomes a sine qua non.